TEACH
TEACH
TEACH

What Is It and How Do I Do It?
10 Keys to Successful Teaching

➤ SANDRA C. CARRANZA ➤

Teach, Teach, Teach
© 2012 by Sandra C. Carranza

Published by Insight International
4739 E. 91st Street, Suite 210
Tulsa, OK 74137
918-493-1718

ISBN: 978-1-890900-75-5

Library of Congress catalog card number: 2012937335

Printed in the United States of America

DEDICATION

I dedicate this book first of all to God the Father who created me in His image and who gave me the heart desire to teach, and who placed in me all that I would need to be an effective teacher.

I dedicate this book secondly to Jesus, the Son of God who gave me eternal life and freedom through His death burial and resurrection.

I dedicate this book thirdly to the Holy Spirit who has strengthened me, lead and guided me, taught me, inspired me, encouraged me, and comforted me all of my life.

I dedicate this book to my husband, Humberto, who has walked with me as one, who has strengthened me by his love and his faith in God and in me.

I dedicate this book to my children, Humberto Esteban, Deborah Elise, Rebekah, and Jesikah Kristine; who gave up their Mom and her time so that others could be affected; who encouraged me when I thought that I had sacrificed them for this calling to teach.

I dedicate this book to my Mom, who was not only a mother to me, but to my children and spouse as I fulfilled the call of God on my life.

I dedicate this book to my siblings Patty, Gene, and Raymond who have helped to shape who I am.

I dedicate this book to my grandchildren (currently Matthew, Armani, Ava and Nathan); it is for your future that I desire to train great teachers.

I dedicate this book to all of the many teachers and students I have taught, that encouraged me by actually implementing what I taught them, and came back to thank me for the difference it made.

I dedicate this book to my pastors Charles and Rochelle Nieman, Casey and Wendy Treat, Art and Kuna Sepulveda, and Drs. Idilio and Rosa Maria Pardillo whom God used to teach, encourage, and mold me through their excellent example and wisdom; and to John Avila who discipled me when I was a new Christian.

I dedicate this book to Dr. Don Petry who inspired me through his personal commitment to education, and who taught me many valuable principles.

Lastly, I dedicate this book to my friends and colleagues who read it, edited it, and translated it; Helen Escobedo, Adrian Ortega, and Kary Pardillo.

CONTENTS

INTRODUCTION

I am a person whose passion is teaching – teaching children, teaching teens, teaching young adults, teaching adults, teaching the elderly. Teaching what? It does not matter what – reading, math, languages, history, science, moral principles, cooking, anything. I love teaching!

Unfortunately, I cannot say that I have loved learning nearly as much. Many of the learning environments that I have been exposed to from elementary to graduate school have failed to cause excitement in me about learning. What a statement coming from someone who has spent the majority of her life in schools! You might ask why the majority of people do not enjoy learning or being in school. I believe that it is because our teachers have not been taught some of the essential principles of teaching. Our colleges and universities have done well in presenting ideas about teaching and information about the learners and learning, but our learning institutions frequently have not taught teachers the actual skills necessary to become great teachers. Though we must take into consideration the fact that teaching experience helps to make great teachers, I firmly believe that we could better prepare entry level teachers with some very important skills which would make them great teachers even in their very first year of teaching.

The purpose of this book is to do exactly that – teach teachers the skills that are needed to be not average, not good, but great teachers. Whether you are a teacher or are studying to be one, the techniques and principles that we will learn from this book will help our students to love learning more than they ever have. We will improve our teaching skills and thus greatly influence our students' learning and their love for learning. The ideas, principles, and skills we will master will help us to experience the great rewards of teaching, help us to love our vocation even more, fulfill our desire to truly teach, and impact our students' lives in a positive way!

In this book, we will treat teaching as a vocation; certainly not as a job, and not as a profession like any other. This book is for those of us who know that our destiny, our mission, our calling is to shape the lives of others. It is written to insure that our teaching experience reaches its highest potential. Considering the magnitude and the importance of this calling or mission to form and develop future generations, teachers deserve to be taught, and must be taught the highest skills possible; then we can be effective in helping our students accomplish their life missions with the greatest degree of success possible.

The key points will be listed at the beginning of each chapter. This will help get us interested in the topics covered in each chapter, and will help us review what we have read. The key points will be introduced in bold, italicized print. At the end of each chapter will be a bold and italicized sub-heading entitled "Wisdom" (application). The best use of this book will be to read through the book once learning and understanding the concepts of each chapter. Then, once you are actually teaching a class, re-read one chapter per month, incorporating the "application" suggestions and evaluating their effects on your class. I believe that this book will be an exciting journey of discovering some essential keys to successful teaching. I am hoping that the "application" exercises will make each one of us great (not just good) teachers. I am eager to share the concepts that I have learned in thirty plus glorious years of teaching and hope that you will be motivated to put them into practice! Enjoy!

Sandra Carranza

Chapter One

TEACH, TEACH, TEACH – WHAT IS IT AND WHY DO IT?

Key Points

1. *Teaching is not a profession or a job – it is a calling and a vocation!*
2. *Teaching requires learning – if my students do not learn, I have not taught!*
3. *Teaching has three aspects – knowledge, understanding, and the ultimate goal, wisdom: applying or doing what you learned.*
4. *Chosen teachers meet six requirements:*
   a. *They are willing (Here I am, use me).*
   b. *They give their lives for their students.*
   c. *They are motivated by love and compassion for their students.*
   d. *They are taken captive by this vocation (Teach or die!).*
   e. *They are prepared (Study to show themselves approved).*
   f. *They are anointed or are yielded to the "Master Teacher".*

I must begin this chapter with an apology as I know that you want to learn the skills necessary to be a successful teacher. Nevertheless, it is important to begin by laying a firm foundation about the "what and why" of teaching, or the vision and philosophy of teaching. Once we have laid this very important foundation, we will learn some very important teaching skills which we will lay on this foundation. I commit that we will dive into some very exciting teaching "how to's" in all of the remaining chapters. Because we want to battle the enemy of average and even good in order to become great teachers, we will spend some time in this chapter internalizing what teaching is and why we do it. This chapter will provide us with a solid foundation upon which we will add the skills necessary to teach effectively. Add to that some practice of these skills, and we are destined to become great teachers with the potential to influence our students and transform the world!

Let us talk about this thing called teaching. First, what is teaching? Teaching is absolutely one of the most important, if not the most important, vocations on the earth. According to Webster's original unabridged dictionary, a vocation is an occupation that is seen by those who carry it out as offering more than simply financial reward; it can also be used to describe any occupation for which a person is specifically gifted, and usually implies that the individual has a form of "calling" for the task. Notice that I do not use the word "occupation", (the principal activity or job that earns money for a person). Why not use that term?

IS TEACHING A JOB, A PROFESSION, OR A VOCATION?

Though teacher schedules, holidays and summer vacations sound desirable; when comparing the work and effort with the pay, we will probably agree that teaching may not be a great job or occupation. Is it a profession which yields prestige, major monetary rewards and security? Again, we would have to say, probably not. Then why would any individual desire to spend their days working with twenty to thirty six year olds, a hundred and fifty teenagers, or a thousand college students, and their nights preparing to do so? The only thing that could possibly motivate one to be a teacher has to be a true calling to do so, or a vocation. Something inside of us tells us that we can make a difference, and we are gifted with the ability to make that difference in the lives of our students. Though teaching can come with many challenges and many discouraging moments, though we are not always able to reach every single student, true teachers live with the hope that they can help to mold their students and therefore change the world. This calling is motivated by sincere love and concern for our students, and fueled with a passion to create positive change in the lives of students and thus in the world in which we live.

CALLED OR CHOSEN?

Let's talk more about this calling All of us have certain gifts and talents to use as we go about doing what we were placed on the earth to do. (I Cor. 7:17). We are all equipped and "called" to do great things on the earth. Unfortunately, many are called to do great things, but few are chosen to do them (Matthew 22:14). How do we become those teachers that are chosen to really make a difference in the lives of others? First of all, we must be willing to answer the call. If I am offering a hundred dollars, or a thousand, or more, I can only give it to those who step up and say, "Yes, I want that." Just like Samuel (I Sam. 3:8), and Isaiah (Isaiah 6:8), we must step up and say,

"Here I am, use me, send me." Chosen teachers step forward and make themselves available to be used.

Secondly, we must be willing to give our lives for our students. The love we have for our students will cause us to lay down our lives for them (John 15:13). As we do this, we will actually find real life and experience the fulfillment of such because he who finds his life will lose it, but he who loses his life for Christ's sake will find it. (Mat. 10:39) There is no greater reward or level of fulfillment for someone who is "called" and "chosen" to teach than to see the results of putting the lives of one's students in front of our own ego's and desires and then to see them flourish. Though we unfortunately do not get to see the fruit and growth in our students in only one year or one college semester, over the years, we are sometimes privy to the amazing influence that our short season with our students had.

Thirdly, those called and chosen to be teachers must be moved by love and compassion for their students just as Jesus was (Matt. 15:32). Only teachers who truly care will be effective in molding the lives of students. Since love never fails (I Cor. 13:8), another requirement of called and chosen teachers is that we truly love our students so much that we are totally committed to the vocation (calling) of teaching them. In a sense, we must be taken captive by the "call". "Called" and "chosen" teachers have an internal sense that we must teach or "die". Philippians 3:13 notes that we must be totally apprehended or taken captive by our call. It cannot be a matter of convenience; it must be "what we do!"

In addition, chosen teachers must be prepared. It is not enough to be called and to answer the call and to be chosen; we must also study to show ourselves approved (II Tim. 2:15). If we were going into surgery, would we prefer a surgeon or would a butcher suffice to do the job? What is the difference, they both use a knife? The difference is preparation. Teachers must continuously study not only the subjects they teach, but the nature of their students and the methods to teach them with. In order to teach, we ourselves must be lifetime learners. We must guard ourselves from the rut that years of experience can sometimes get us in, and always be interested in learning new techniques and skills that will help us be better teachers. In the teaching field, we really cannot ever say that we have arrived. As society changes, so do students, and we will have to adjust to those changes in our techniques, and take full advantage of what is available to us now, that was not available a few years ago. My point here is that we must continuously be open to learning. We should look forward to staff development days not as a day off without our students, but as opportunities to continue to become and to remain great teachers.

Lastly, called and chosen teachers must have the anointing or the gift or the talent working in them as they teach (Isaiah 10:27). The ability to rely on that gift, talent, guide, and ability placed in us by the Holy Spirit makes all of the difference in the world when we are teaching. This is how we get strength in weakness (I Cor. 12:10). One of my best years of teaching was my first year teaching in a Christian School. I was asked to teach a combination class of fifth and sixth graders, and I started in November! I had at least four students with severe learning and behavioral issues, and was a new Christian. Throughout that year, I was amazed as the Holy Spirit taught me to teach and to reach them! Many years of experience and study have confirmed that I was actually using sound, educationally proven, effective teaching techniques. Since that time, I have taught all ages of students, and all subjects from phonics to English to algebra and geometry; and many students have actually asked if I would please continue as the permanent teacher of the class. My point here is that when we are called and chosen, we have the "Master Teacher" living on the inside of us who if given the opportunity, will make us the greatest teachers on earth!

I do recognize that though the teaching profession is considered poorly remunerated, there are some perks. Many have entered this field because of the attractive daily schedule, the enticing three month summer vacation and three additional weeks of vacation at Christmas and Easter, and even the possibly less challenging university course load. I would hope to convince those who entered for these reasons, that teaching is a vital, life changing, world influencing profession. For those who sincerely believe that teaching is what they were created to do, who desire to teach effectively, and who sincerely have a yearning to change the lives of many, and prepare individuals who will impact positively and dramatically the world and community they live in; I hope to establish, strengthen, settle, and help to equip you with this book.

WHAT IS TEACHING?

What exactly is teaching? Some say it is imparting knowledge; others say it is guiding others as they discover knowledge; still others would say it is molding and training; it is to cause to learn, to instruct. Yes, it is all of the above and more! According to Webster, teaching is to: counsel and direct; suggest to the mind; impress on the mind; accustom or make familiar with; communicate or tell; give instruction and show; admonish and guide; manage and direct; give intelligence or impart knowledge. How exciting, how complex, how large!

Yet, teaching is still more. Teaching is preparing others to reach their God given destiny; it is helping others to grow and mature so that they can be the great people God created them to be, and so that they can accomplish the great things He created them to accomplish! It is giving them the skills to do great and mighty exploits! It is empowering them with the confidence that they can do what they were created to do. Teaching is far more than giving facts and information and knowledge; it is loving and believing in an individual more than they believe in themselves, and thus touching a life and the world for eternity.

DOES TEACHING REQUIRE LEARNING?

In discussing what teaching is, we must consider an important principle and the answer to the following questions. Does teaching require learning? If my students do not learn, did I really teach? Is their learning my responsibility? I would like to propose this concept: if I truly teach, then my students learn; and the opposite: if my students do not learn, I do not really teach. As teachers, we must be willing to take some responsibility for the end result. We must have our minds and hearts set on making a difference and causing change. What a joy to be able to say, "My students learned; therefore I taught", instead of, "I taught, if they did not learn, I am sorry."

One might ask, "How much responsibility does the student have regarding learning, and is all of the responsibility on the teacher?" I believe that the degree of teacher verses student responsibility for learning lessens as the student matures as a learner. When a child is born, one hundred percent of the responsibility belongs to his first teachers – his parents. As he matures as a learner, he must take more and more responsibility for his learning. During the first three or four years of formal education, about ninety percent of the responsibility still lies with the teacher. If the student is in class, and has the maturity and ability to focus, and the teacher takes responsibility for teaching and has the skills to do so, then he will probably learn (barring a problem with processing or some other exceptional learning need). As the student progresses through the upper elementary grades, he assumes additional responsibility for learning; just being in class and attending will not suffice. The student will have to do more, and the percentage of teacher responsibility decreases to about seventy percent. From junior high through the last year of high school, that percentage will probably move from seventy to fifty percent. Meaning that a senior in high school should depend upon the teacher for fifty percent of what he actually learns. From post-secondary through doctorate, the responsibility for learning should progress to ninety percent student and ten percent teacher. These percentages are not based on scientific data, and of course each learner will progress at his own level, but the following chart will give us a general idea. Please note that even at the highest levels of education, we will always need a teacher, and learner maturity and responsibility for learning have a direct relationship.

Learner	%Teacher / Student Responsibility
Infant (0-3)	100/0
Pre-school (4-5)	90/10
Primary (6-8) (G1-3)	80/20
Upper Elem. (9-11) (G4-6)	70/30
Intermediate (12-14) (G7-9)	60/40
High School (15-17) (G10-12)	50/50
Bachelors	40/60
Masters	20/80
Doctorate	10/90

Some teachers might have the philosophy that we cannot make a student learn and therefore their learning is not our responsibility. We all know the saying, "You can lead a horse to water, but you cannot make him drink." It is true; we cannot make that horse drink, but we can put so much salt in his food that he will want to drink. We cannot make our students learn, but if we can establish this principle (If my students do not learn, I have not taught), and learn the skills of teaching (those techniques that will make them "thirsty"), our students will learn, and we will have truly taught.

KNOWLEDGE, UNDERSTANDING AND WISDOM

As we lay the important foundation upon which we will add the skills necessary for effective teaching, it is important to consider three very important elements of teaching: knowledge, understanding, and wisdom. I am ever thankful to Dr. Don Petry, former president of the University of Missouri, founding president of Regents University, and president of Teled International, an organization which has assisted in starting and in strengthening numerous schools in countries all over the world, for offering me his insights into these three key elements. An entire book could be written about them, but I will attempt to briefly explain them since the knowledge, understanding, and application of these three elements are crucial to the foundation we must have before we learn the skills involved with effective teaching.

We can define knowledge as information and facts. When we attach meaning or comprehension to that information or those facts, we have understanding. Finally wisdom is the ability and the will to act upon the knowledge and the understanding of those facts and that information. Many teachers focus primarily on knowledge and understanding, but often do not concern themselves with the ability and desire of our students to implement or act upon the knowledge we give them. Actually, a focus on applying what is learned moves our teaching from being "interesting" or "good," to being relevant and life changing. Teaching which considers all three of these elements will actually cause students to do something with what they learn, and thus our teaching will influence the world which each one of our students goes into.

Teaching is not just reading to the class what is in a book. Teaching is not just having students read what is in a book. It is taking knowledge and breaking it down into a format that students can understand. Then it is giving them the opportunity to practice that knowledge over and over until they are able to put that knowledge into action. Finally, it is helping them to apply that knowledge over and over until it becomes something they can do without even thinking about it. In the following chapters of this book, you will learn how to teach to accomplish this. After all, teaching does require learning.

WHY TEACH?

Why teach? A well-known actor once said, "Behind every famous, great, successful person is a fantastic teacher". This statement holds true in every field; a teacher helps to provide an individual with faith in themselves and their gifting; then teaches those skills that are necessary for success in that profession; then takes the learner through consistent practice of those skills until they are mastered. Jesus Christ, the Savior of the world, was a teacher. His teachings revolutionized the world. He was indeed the "Master Teacher". He was so successful with his first students (disciples) that His teachings (the Gospel) continue to be taught to this day, over two thousand years after His death! As teachers, we can influence the quality of an individual's life; alter the course of an individual's life; and even impact the future by influencing the students we teach! Why teach? Teach because it makes a difference in lives, in our communities, in our world!

TO SUMMARIZE

Teaching is more than a mere job. It is the response and commitment to a special "calling" and "gift" placed on an individual's life by God. When one has this gift and this calling, there is an innate ability and a strong desire to teach, which must be accompanied by a "Here am I, send me" attitude. When this response and attitude are coupled with the motivating factor of love, the teaching vocation not only yields an incredible amount of fulfillment (the joy of being overwhelmingly content and satisfied with what one is doing as a vocation!) it yields true fruit (individuals who take what they have learned and apply it to the world that they live in)!

Unfortunately, there is another thing that can keep true teachers from being fulfilled; this is the lack of training in teaching skills. It will be our goal in the following chapters to learn or review some of those vital teaching skills which will result in us being truly great teachers. In each of the following chapters, we will not only get knowledge, but add understanding to that knowledge, and then have opportunities to actually apply or practice (wisdom) what we learn. I am looking forward to each chapter in our quest to defeat average and become great!

APPLICATION (WISDOM)

1. *In only one paragraph, write in your own words your vision and philosophy of education. Place a copy of this what and why in front of every week of lesson plans, and read it before you plan each week.*

2. *When writing weekly lesson plans, along with teaching objectives, note knowledge with a "K", note activities that promote understanding with a "U", and note activities that encourage wisdom or application with a "W".*

3. *Insure that for every concept taught (knowledge and understanding); ample time is given for applying (wisdom) what has been learned.*

Chapter Two

TOUCHING HEARTS TO TOUCH MINDS

Key Points

1. *Connecting and relating to our students by touching their hearts first, will then help our students to open their minds to what we teach.*

2. *External impressions of our internal qualities such as friendliness, professionalism, strength, courage, and wisdom will help our students want to learn from us.*

3. *We can establish a relationship of trust by seeing, speaking, and believing in what our students will become.*

4. *Blessing our students with meaningful touches, spoken messages, expressions of high value, desire for a special future, and commitment will touch our students' hearts so that they will allow us to touch their minds.*

Teach, Teach, Teach, What is it and how do I do it? In the last chapter, we defined teaching as a vocation (not a profession and not a job), which requires a calling and a willingness to answer that calling. Then we established that through teaching, we can impact not only the lives of students, but we can also impact our world through the influence that we can have on each of our students. We discussed the three levels of teaching (knowledge, understanding and wisdom), and our need to have students act (wisdom) on what we give them, instead of just accumulating facts (knowledge).

In order to accomplish true teaching, the foundational key of trust must be laid, and this will be the topic of this chapter. A relationship of trust between us and our students must be established before we will really be able to teach them. This trust can be gained by relating to them, by connecting with them, by demonstrating our commitment to them, by physically touching them, by verbalizing our sincere love and faith in them, and by putting them at ease with us. No matter how old our students are, no learning can take place until our students first trust us. The younger our students are and the less experience they have had with teachers, the easier it will be for us to gain this "trust". The older our students are and the more experiences they have had with an unfriendly educational environment or with lack of success in school, the harder it will be to gain this "trust".

A RELATIONSHIP OF TRUST IS NECESSARY IN ORDER TO TEACH

I strongly believe that our students will not open their minds and much less their lives to us until we have first touched their hearts. A teacher's sincere and heartfelt love and concern for his or her students sets the stage for this trust relationship. Brain research describes a mechanism in the brain that allows the brain to receive information only after a sense of well-being and comfort has been established. According to Vygotsky, "...all the higher functions originate as actual relations between human individuals." (1978, p.57). In other words, relationships with others cause the higher functions of the brain to operate. This might explain the fact that even though sometimes we as teachers are well qualified to teach our subject matter, some students will say, "I just cannot learn from this teacher." One reason might be that the teacher's teaching technique and methodology needs work, but another might be that we have not opened that brain mechanism by establishing a relationship of trust with the student. You might say, "But I am not a relational, touchy, feely type of person." Maybe not, but relational skills and techniques can be learned just as we can all learn to ride a bicycle, or to drive a car, or to cook. Given the right training, and practice, we are all capable of learning to relate to our students and thus promoting success in teaching them. I have heard it said that 90% of our success in life in general depends on our people skills, and only 10% on our knowledge. Learning the skills and techniques of putting our students at ease and helping them want to learn from us will be the focus of this chapter. Remember the old saying, "You can lead a horse to water, but you can't make him drink." One of the ways to make a horse drink is to put salt in his oats. I believe the same is true with students and learning. We cannot make them learn, but we can certainly do some things that will help them want to learn and to learn from us as their teachers.

Have you ever heard the saying that a disciple (student) is not higher than his teacher and that when he (the student) is fully trained, he will be just like his teacher? (Luke 6:40). As a school administrator of more than twenty five years, I have seen this principle hold true, year after year. I had the pleasure of having a Hawaiian kindergarten teacher in our school. She was so calm and so kind and loving, and no matter what the personality of her class or her students was, it was wonderful to see how they became just like her within a few weeks of school. Her students became as soft spoken as she was. They became kind and so loving towards each other due to her beautiful "aloha" spirit. I had another kindergarten teacher who was strong and bold, and very "down to business", and again, within a few weeks, I could see these characteristics in her students. Each teacher has the privilege of adding something to the lives of each one of his or her students. I believe that students make a decision (unconsciously and sometimes even consciously) to learn from a particular teacher. After all, when all is said and done, they will be just like their teacher. Are our students choosing not to allow us to teach them because they do not want to be just like us? You see, it is up to them whether they will consider us their teacher (allow us to teach them) and become just like us; therefore, it is up to us to be teachers that they desire to emulate.

EXTERNAL IMPRESSIONS

Let's begin with first impressions. Before we get to say anything to our students, they will make some predeterminations based on what they see. You might say, "That is not right!" I agree that it isn't, but nevertheless, it is a fact that first impressions are very important regarding whether our students will allow us to be their teachers... Therefore, let's examine our outward appearance – our calling card and the first impression that will speak very loudly to our students before we get a chance to utter our first words of introduction to them. When our students look at us, will they desire to be just like us? We might say, "Just like me, oh my!" Or can we say "Just like me, great!" If they are going to learn from us, they must be able to look at us and desire to be like us. If they look at us, and do not desire to be like us, then they make a decision not to allow us to be their teacher, and really will not learn from us. Think about this, would you listen to and learn from, a fitness trainer who was obviously fifty pounds overweight, smoking a cigarette and eating pizza dripping with grease? Probably not! There is great wisdom in the saying, "...By this time you ought to be teachers yourselves, yet here I find you need someone to sit down with you and go over the basics on God again, starting from square one..." (Hebrews 5:12, Message Bible). This scripture may make us a little uncomfortable, but as teachers we must have a high standard. We do not have to be perfect to be teachers, but as those who impart knowledge and understanding and wisdom, we too must be eager to improve. To improve, just means to change, and if we think about it, everything that is still living is always changing; when we stop changing, we stop living. So, with that said, let's take a look at ourselves, both inward and outward as it relates to establishing connections with our students.

Still dealing with first impressions, let's first consider our countenance. In my own life, I have often been told that people are afraid of me when they first meet me. Once they get to know me and know my heart, they are comfortable with me, but with many people all I have is that first impression. With this knowledge and understanding that my facial expressions or even posture or gestures could be keeping others from being at ease with me and thus hindering their trust relationship with me, I have made a decision to act accordingly (wisdom: the application of knowledge and understanding), or learn and practice a skill which will help me overcome this problem. Even though my face does not smile naturally (some people's faces actually turn down naturally), I can indeed smile if I think about it and determine to do it. I am one of those people who will have to purposely glue a smile on my face and show my teeth or be misinterpreted as being stern or angry or unapproachable. Therefore, skill number one regarding external impressions is to smile, and smile and smile some more. A smile is contagious and it puts others at ease. It also demonstrates our own confidence in ourselves, and this helps others feel confident trusting in us. In addition, a smile says, "It's alright, come on over, I am approachable," whereas a stern face says, "Stay away." So, the first skill we have learned is to smile and smile some more, telling our students that everything is fine and that they can trust us.

The next skill regards our appearance. Is our appearance really that important in connecting with our students? I really think it is. Our clothing and grooming will either attract our students to us or cause them to reject us. I will use myself as an example. The way that I carry myself, my facial expressions, and even the speed of my walk can make people uncomfortable and intimidated. Add a black business suit to this, and I would seem very unapproachable. Therefore, not only do I have to glue that smile on my face, slow down, be cautious of my arm and hand gestures, but I must also drape myself in clothing and colors that are warm and feminine. What about a teacher who goes to school in an oversized shirt and worn jeans? Or what about the one who goes to school in polyester pants, a collared shirt buttoned to the top and a plastic pencil holder in his front pocket? Or what about the teacher who wears "flip-flops" and a "tent" dress? Does our attire really make any difference in whether our students desire to learn from us or not? I do believe that our appearance can help our students respect us and desire to be like us, or that it could cause students to reject us and ultimately what we have to teach them. I would suggest that we dress professionally; a good rule of thumb might be to dress just one level higher than the dress code for our students. You might say, "I want to look just like them so that they can relate to me". In order for our students to relate to us as their teachers, not as their "buddies", we cannot dress just like them. This is especially true of those who teach at the junior high, high school and even post-secondary levels. We want to be comfortable, make our students comfortable, and at the same time give our students something to look up to, and hopefully not down on. Now we have learned two things that we can do to help our students want to be taught by us: keeping a warm and encouraging smile on our faces, and working on an outward appearance that students can look up to and even desire to emulate.

THE EXPRESSION OF INTERNAL QUALITIES

Of course, outward appearance is not everything; it is just the first impression. Let's talk about some even more important aspects that attract or retract students; those internal qualities that our students see in us. Students will be attracted to teachers who have strength and courage, and they will take advantage of teachers who demonstrate weakness and fear. Though being a great teacher does not require a dominant personality, teachers must understand that they are in authority and that their students must be under that authority. Understanding the principle of authority is also crucial to having good class control. We can be in authority without being harsh or authoritarian or mean. Strength and courage are outward evidences that we understand that we are the experts in the classroom and that we are in command. Our students and people in general, desire to follow a strong leader and courageous leader. The followers of Joshua as he became the leader after Moses' death required one thing of him, "...that he be strong and of good courage." (Joshua 1:18) Though this is a very challenging goal to reach for, when we recognize that strength and courage are both decisions that we make and not necessarily qualities that we are born with, it is easier for us to exhibit these qualities.

We must be that leader in the classroom, or one of our students will become that leader. It is important to know who we are and to exhibit strength and courage in front of our students. And when we do not feel so bold or strong or courageous, I like to quote Mamie McCullough, one of Zig Ziglar's protégées, "Just fake it until you make it!" Believe me, our students will never know the difference, and they will feel secure with us and really open their minds to our teaching.

Another externally evident characteristic of attractive teachers is their wisdom. Again, our students, and people in general, desire to follow those who are wise. Even young children know what wisdom is and what foolishness is. They know when we are doing what we are supposed to do and when we are not. They know when we are following our leader and when we are not. In general, our students seek wise teachers; we remember that wisdom is "applying" the knowledge and understanding that we have obtained. We could say that students will be attracted to teachers who practice what we teach. The old saying, "Do as I say, not as I do" has never been effective. We must demonstrate wisdom, and when we miss the mark, we must admit it, and allow our students to see how we learn and grow from our mistakes. There is a truthful saying, "Even a fool is considered wise when he holds his tongue." What we say must be in agreement with what we are teaching, and then what we are doing must be in agreement with that. When we are able to do this, then our students will want to be taught by us.

Other qualities that our students will seek in us are love, joy, peace, patience, kindness, goodness, faithfulness, gentleness, and self-control (Gal. 5:22). It is not necessary to discuss each of these qualities in detail as they are each self-explanatory. It is sufficient to say that any one or all of these qualities would be assets to us as we attempt to attract our students to us. Of course, the opposites of these fruits would result in our students rejecting us and not allowing us to truly teach them.

ESTABLISHING A RELATIONSHIP OF TRUST

Now that we are working on being those teachers our students want to be like, let us look at some areas that will help our students begin to trust us. When we look back on our own lives searching for those teachers who made a difference in our lives, which teachers make the list? Usually, they are those who really loved us and believed in us, and who challenged us to do more than we thought we could. First, let's discuss being teachers who love their students. We have been given the ability to love even the unlovable students with the unconditional love of God (Rom. 5:5). We must decide daily to love our students even when we do not love what they do. Loving someone is demonstrated through our words and our actions. It will help our students and ourselves if we begin with words. Saying that we love them will first help us to believe that we do, and will actually begin to change our actions. We all desire to please those who love us and those whom we love. As our students hear that we love them, they will also change their actions into those that will please us. Today's society has taught us to guard our love talk and our love walk because they could be mistaken for ulterior motives, but, we cannot allow this to stop us from expressing our unconditional love to our students both in words and actions.

SEEING, SPEAKING, AND BELIEVING IN WHAT OUR STUDENTS WILL BE BECOME

One demonstration of our love for our students is our ability to have a vision for them not as they are at this moment, but as they will be in both the immediate and ultimate future. We have to see those first graders, reading, writing, functioning in a structured environment from the first day of school. We have to see our high school and college students fulfilling their God given destinies while they are yet students. As teachers, we must exercise the God given ability to see the end from the beginning and to see the end also when each day along the way does not look like the end. We do have this ability because we were made in the image of God, and just like Him, we are not moved by sight, but by faith (II Cor. 5:7). This "seeing" combines with speaking and believing to help build young people who accomplish great things with their lives. Since the eye is the light of the body, our ability to see the end result lights the path of our students to arrive at their destinations. If our eye is good, then their lives will be good, but if our eye is evil, then we cannot help light the paths of their lives. As teachers, we must have good eyesight; good vision for our students. This vision is for the first week of school, for the first quarter, for the entire year, and even for the final plans God has for their lives.

A great way to hold on to the vision for our class or for our individual students is to write it. Habakkuk 2:2 says to write the vision and make it plain so that whoever reads it can run with it. This passage states that someone reads the vision, and infers that when they hear it, they can run with it or accomplish it. That is where the speaking of it over our students comes in. As we speak it both to ourselves and to them, we will create faith which means to believe. In order to believe, we must speak, and that speaking will enhance believing both on our part and on our students' parts. Knowing that a teacher believes in you will make you want to learn from them. Finding a teacher who will help you to believe in you will make our students want to open their lives and their hearts to us.

For those of us who may have some difficulty with this "speaking of the vision", I would like to share one of the most important things I learned that revolutionized my relationships with my family, my students, and with people in general. Learning and practicing certain skills will eventually enable us to be good at them. For example, I am not a painter, but if someone taught me some skills, I could become one. Even though painting is not my gift and I could never be a Michelangelo, I could paint a decent picture. Likewise, I may not be good at complimenting and speaking great words over my students, but if I can learn the skill and practice it, I can become good at this action that does not come naturally to me. Dr. Gary Smalley refers to this ability of seeing and speaking and causing us and our students to believe the vision as the "blessing" in his book entitled, *The Blessing*. I highly recommend that every sincere and serious teacher striving to be great read this book. It should be required reading for every teacher and parent. Now, not everyone grew up with a blessing (having someone see and speak good things about us), so we are not all good at giving a blessing (seeing and speaking good things about others). Nevertheless, it is absolutely essential that we receive a blessing (having someone see and speak good things about us) in order to be successful in life. Everyone needs a blessing (others who will believe in them and help them to believe in themselves).

THE BLESSING (SEEING AND SPEAKING GOOD THINGS ABOUT OTHERS)

Giving a "blessing" is one of those skills that can be learned, just like gluing that smile on our faces. The "blessing" is very prevalent in the Bible, and the book by Dr. Smalley describes its components. I will summarize the main techniques here, but nothing will take the place of reading his book. The components will be easy to learn and understand, but we must remember that wisdom is actually applying what we learn. To become skilled at giving "blessings", we will have to practice, but they will make a large difference in the lives of our students and help us to be effective teachers. The techniques we will discuss and then practice are:

- → Meaningful touch
- → Spoken message
- → High value
- → Vision for a special future
- → Commitment

A MEANINGFUL TOUCH

The first skill involves a physical touch. Studies show that everyone needs at least eight to ten meaningful touches per day. Again, the world has made us a little paranoid about touching each other, and most teachers are very cautious about touching their students. Though we must be guarded not to give the wrong impression when touching our students, how about a pat (not a massage) on the back or shoulder, a side hug, a hand shake, or even a flick of the hair or a pat on the head? Patients whose doctors sit on their beds and make some physical contact with them actually heal faster than patients whose doctors stand at the foot of their beds and never make contact. No wonder God placed over one third of the feeling receptors in the hands. Studies have proven that there are physiological benefits to touching; hemoglobin levels increase, body tissues receive more oxygen, and we are energized and regenerated because of touch. Now you might ask, "How do I give my students meaningful touches in a way that I will not be misunderstood"?

How about standing at the door and touching each student as they enter or leave the classroom? We could pat them on the shoulder, or shake their hand, or even give them a side hug. We could flip their hair, or pat their head (careful with the "do" of a high schooler). We could "high five" them, or "low five" them. The key is to get them a meaningful touch from a significant person in their life. Would these actions demonstrate some type of care, love and concern? You might be wondering what the response of our students might be. Younger students will generally respond positively to meaningful touches, older students and students who have received little "stroking" will be uncomfortable at first, and may even avoid "touches". If you yourself feel very uncomfortable with this, it is probably because you also never received this type of "blessing" as a child or even as an adult. Practice makes perfect as they say. You may have to try this one out on your loved ones first, before you would even consider it with your students, but believe me; it will make a positive difference in establishing a trusting relationship with your students and with others.

Remember that everyone needs eight to ten meaningful touches every day.

I hesitantly add a caution here. As I stated earlier, with all of the sexual and physical abuse that has occurred in society, it has almost become taboo to touch anyone! Physical contact with our students must be non-threatening and very pure. Respect those students who respond negatively to physical contact. You may have to gain their trust with spoken words before you can try this important technique. Hugs should be from side to side, and from the shoulders up. Never touch a student whom you are correcting! Never touch a student in a way that your motives might be questioned, and avoid ever being alone with any student. It would be safer to advise teachers never to touch a student, but so much would be lost if we played it safe. Therefore, proceed with caution, but do proceed.

A SPOKEN MESSAGE

The second part of the blessing is a "spoken message", and I did say spoken. Since most people never had anyone say good things about them, they find it difficult to do so, or they feel uncomfortable when someone says something nice about them. We ask, "What would they think of me?" "This feels awkward", we say. Or "What does this person want from me," we think. Most people believe that others know how we feel, without us having to say it. They think that because we said it once, or because we do things for others that they will know how we feel. Unfortunately this is not the case. Is it enough for a husband who tells his wife he loves her on their wedding day to expect this statement to last the entire marriage? Or is the fact that he goes to work daily to financially support the family a good enough indicator of his love? What about us as teachers? The things we do and even the sacrifices we make will not suffice. We must tell our students that we care, and we must tell them often.

As teachers, we must always be digging for gold; looking for opportunities to speak good things about our students. When we do, our students actually wait for our words as one would wait for the rain in a drought. Instead of turning us off, our students will desire to hear us because we speak positive words that encourage and please them. When we tell one student how much we appreciate their attention or hard work or obedience, all of our other students follow because they also desire a "blessing". Practice these blessings: I love you, you are my best class, you are so intelligent, and I know you will do great things, you can do this, you are so obedient, you have such excellent spirits, and you work so hard, I admire your strength; you have the gift of words, etc...

ATTACHING HIGH VALUE

When our students know that we value them, they want to be around us, and they will accept us as their teachers. Wouldn't we all rather be around someone who really values us and likes us than around someone who does not? Attaching high value to our students will take some practice and some skill development, but I will show you how. First, we study our students and easily see their strengths. Then, we look for an ordinary object that reminds us of this strength, and finally, we speak this over that student. This part of the blessing was often spoken in the Bible, and was considered a permanent and powerful blessing. Jesus called Peter a "rock", even before he was one. God called Abraham "father" when he had no children.

Let's try this with our students. What about that "diamond", who shines and is so bright, yet so sharp that she can cut? How about that "tower of strength" that others seem to lean on? And what of that "ant" that is smaller than everyone, but never stops, and needs no overseer, and carries three times his weight? And the "glue" that keeps everyone working together? Are you getting the picture? I am not suggesting that on the first day of class you give everyone a new name. But, as you get to know your students, encourage them by attaching high value to them by using this technique. This will be another key to gaining their trust, and to having a positive influence on their lives.

A SPECIAL FUTURE

We can become quite proficient at the art of taking those characteristics of our students which challenge us and turning them into blessings. This component is called picturing a special future for our students. After all, God created them and placed in each one of them certain gifts and abilities and qualities; those that will be necessary for them to accomplish His great plan for their lives. For example, consider the student that just cannot stop talking, no matter where or who they are seated next to. Could it be that that gift of "gab", which quite bothers his or her teachers, will be what will open the door for them to be a great politician, or actor, or mediator? Could it be that the student who must constantly be in motion will become a professional athlete or a famous dancer? And what about that student who takes such a long time to respond because he must think through every detail first, could he be the discoverer of the cure of a serious disease or inventor of something that will aid us in dealing with natural disasters?

You see, we have a choice; we can take that quality and express it in negative terms, or we can take it and use the power of our words to encourage our students and build their self-esteem and confidence. Here is an example. We have all had students who seem to know everything that is going on in everyone's lives. We could call them gossipers and busy bodies, or we could speak a blessing over them like this: "You have a natural concern for others; I would not be surprised if you became a counselor or a psychologist, or maybe even a reporter". What about that student that seems to challenge the system and the rules and even the teacher? Do we call him rebellious and stubborn, or can we speak a blessing understanding that this is his natural bent? His blessing would go something like this: "You have such strong convictions, and you see things black or white; you would make a great judge, or lawyer". How about these: "You are very careful and accurate, and like to take your time, I would definitely trust you with my money or even my life. You love to be funny and to be at the center of attention, acting or teaching might be fun for you".

A COMMITMENT

We must convince our students that we are committed to them for the long term in order to gain their trust and thus the privilege of being their teachers. In addition to those positive words, meaningful touches, high value, and a special future, we can demonstrate to them that we will be there for them when they need us. This will mean that we invest our time and even our resources in our students. It is said that actions speak louder than words, and investing time talking with, tutoring, attending their games, etc... speaks volumes. No, we are not their parents, though to those without, we become that too, but we must be willing to "lay down our lives" for our students. It means that maybe instead of shooting out of school as soon as the bell rings, we stay for those students who did not quite understand a concept, or that we sit with the parents of a student to see how we can reach that student as we work together, or maybe even take the time to speak with a colleague about what has worked with this particular student. You may be saying, "What about my own family?" Of course, we must always keep our priorities in line, but I have found that what I have done for another's child, someone has done for my children when they are in need.

We can also demonstrate our commitment to our students by making the effort to study them, their personality bents, and their interests. Maybe we have a student who is not successful academically, but he shines in music or art or athletics. Learning about, respecting, and honoring these interests will actually help that student to spark an interest in what we are trying to add to his life. Though I was not an athlete, or that interested in music, learning about football, or who the latest singing groups are has bought me a lot of student attention over the years.

There are so many ways to demonstrate our commitment to our students! The point is that it will take our time and even resources, but the reward is a life that can be changed. I remember a student in jeopardy of not graduating because homework assignments rarely got done. With the permission of his grandparents who he lived with, I had him stay until the homework was done, and if it was time for me to leave, he went home with me and my children and we actually drove him home when the homework was done. The student graduated and today has realized his dream of being a law enforcement agent. He did not care much for academics, but without a high school diploma, he could not be where he is today. I remember teaching an Algebra I class of students who had learning challenges and who could not keep up with the regular class. I would bake chocolate chip cookies for the student who got the highest grade on the test (of course that student always shared with the others). This showed them that I cared, and every one of those students passed Algebra I, and hopefully got a better foundation for the next math class they would take. My commitment to them became their commitment to me. It caused them to allow me to teach them, which is what this chapter is all about.

To summarize, we must first touch our students' hearts before we can touch their minds. Students will not give us the privilege of being their teachers unless we do. We have discussed the various ways to reach their hearts, beginning with our outward countenance, demeanor, and even appearance and including this technique called the "blessing". To reach them, we must speak positive words about them, we must touch them in a pure and meaningful way, we must attach high value to them, we must study them to discover their special future, and we must be committed to stick with them until they reach it. I believe that every person was born to do great and significant things with their lives. Some do fulfill God's plan for their lives, and some do not. I believe that a teacher and a parent have the powerful responsibility and awesome privilege of touching lives to touch the future. In this chapter we have discussed one of the foundational keys to accomplishing that – the key of touching hearts to touch minds, and touching lives to touch the future.

APPLICATION (WISDOM)

1. *Smile, smile, smile! Smile in the classroom, smile in the hall, smile on your way to the office, smile on your way to your car smile all the time! Work on getting rid of intimidating gestures (pointing finger, folded arms, voice too loud, speech too quick, etc...)*

2. *Write these words on index cards: Strength, Courage, Love, Joy, Peace, Patience, Kindness, Goodness, Faithfulness, Gentleness, and Self Control. Pull and place one card in a visible place in your classroom daily or weekly.*

   Attempt to demonstrate the quality to your students.

3. *Select clothing that will earn respect and confidence from your students and colleagues! Do this for one week, and write down what your students and colleagues say.*

4. *Say something positive to every student every day!*

5. *Give as many meaningful touches as your students will allow every day- your goal is eight per student!*

6. *Find an object that will value the strengths of each student; print them and hand them out to each student. Refer to each student by this object at least once a day!*

7. *Picture and speak that special future over each student daily!*

8. *Demonstrate your commitment to those who are still not receptive of you as a teacher one time this week.*

Chapter Three

PREPARE TO TEACH OR PLAN TO FAIL

Key Points

1. *We either plan or prepare to teach, or we have planned to fail.*
2. *We must prepare annually ("Living Curriculum Guide"), weekly (Lesson Plan & Notes and Outlines), and daily (Meditation, Prayer and Positive Confession).*
3. *We are guides, facilitators, we show our students how.*
4. *We give our students knowledge and understanding with which they will be able to think and reason at the higher thinking levels.*
5. *We should always "MIS" and "KIS" (Make it simple and keep it simple)!*

In chapter one, we discussed the "what" and "why" of teaching, the relationship between teaching and learning, and the concepts of knowledge, understanding, and wisdom (applying what is learned). As a part of that strong foundation, in chapter two, we added the key component of establishing a trusting relationship between ourselves and our students in order for them to allow us to teach them. We also discussed the importance of being teachers that our students will desire to emulate, and discussed at length how a "blessing" can greatly enhance this relationship built on trust. With these strong foundations laid, and believing that you have put into practice (wisdom) the skills of relating to your students, let us spend the next few chapters working on skills that every teacher must possess if they are really going to teach.

The teaching process consists of three parts: preparation, instruction, and evaluation or assessment. In this chapter, we will talk about the first part: preparing to teach. I strongly believe that if we do not prepare, we will not truly teach, because as we mentioned in the first chapter, if our students do not learn, then we have not really taught. So, with this in mind, we must prepare or we will not be able to insure that our students do truly learn the material that we teach.

TEACHERS ARE PERPETUAL LEARNERS

One might say, "I spent sixteen years preparing to teach." This is true, but weekly and even daily, we must continue to study and prepare. All professionals must be perpetual learners. Effective and successful medical doctors do not stop studying and preparing when they leave medical school, but continue to keep current with today's diseases, cures, and prevention. Imagine an accountant who never learned to use the new computer software for preparing budgets and tracking finances because he stopped learning when he graduated from college. We as teachers can do no less. In other words, we should be perpetual or life-long learners.

Some of the most common methods of preparation are participating in staff development, reading the most recent studies on education, networking with other teachers, and even returning to college to become a specialist in our major. Often we as teachers are so pressed for time that our attitude about staff development is that we would rather just be given the time in our classrooms to catch up with paper work and prepare for the next day. Likewise often we are so busy completing paper work that we do not have time to read, and that long awaited summer break is needed and used to rest and refuel or spend time with our families. Yet as professionals and ones "chosen" to this vocation, we must be willing to be learners. Remember that when our students have been fully trained, they will become like their teachers. Are we interested in learning, are we continuing our education, and are we life-long students? If so, then our students will be also. Thus the first part of this very important skill of preparation is to be a life-long learner.

FAILING TO PREPARE MEANS PREPARING TO FAIL

In addition to remaining current in the teaching field and in the subjects we teach, we must also maintain an annual, weekly, and daily habit of preparing. I believe that if we fail to prepare, then we have prepared to fail. When we are sure of what we are teaching and how we will reach our objectives, our classes run smoothly, and our students learn. When we are unprepared and are not sure what our objectives are and how we will reach them, it seems that havoc breaks out in our classrooms and not only do our students fail to reach the learning objectives, they are disorderly and difficult to handle. When we "study to show ourselves approved", then we will be teachers who "need not be ashamed of our work." (II Tim. 2:14-16). So, even though we may have taught first grade for twenty years (if so, maybe we need a change to challenge us) or a particular college history course for a long time, we must still prepare or study. What do we mean by preparing? According to Webster, to prepare means to make ones self-ready or to take the necessary previous measures in order to be ready. We have to get ready to teach, and this getting ready includes annual, weekly, and daily preparation. Since it is vitally important for us to prepare for the year, the week and even the day we are teaching, we will discuss each type of preparation separately. Let's begin with preparing for the entire year.

PREPARING FOR THE ENTIRE YEAR

Annual preparation begins before our students ever come on campus and gives us great insight. Our goals or objectives and the milestones along the way to reaching them are clear to us. Our annual planning is similar to that preparation we would make to go on a road trip. We take our map and first pinpoint our current location and then our final destination. Then we carefully plan each stop between, noting how far we will drive, where we will stay, and what sights we will visit. As teachers, we must do the same. To figure out where to start, we must study the objectives of the previous year or pre-requisite course. This tells us where our students are, or at least where they should be. Next, we will note the final objectives for the course or grade we will teach. Then we divide and chart these learning objectives or goals in terms of the periods we will be teaching. For example, elementary periods are usually divided into six, six week periods; junior high and high school into four quarters; and college into semesters. Finally, we will chart the objectives by the weeks; weeks one to six in elementary; weeks one to nine in junior and senior high; and so on.

In our first step of annual preparation we determine where our students are when they come to us; what do they or should they know, what should they have mastered in the previous year or course? This takes looking at the curriculum of the previous year to note what concepts were introduced, reviewed and mastered in the previous course or year. This step will require some research in the grade or courses your students had last year. We will have to borrow the scope and sequence for the pre-requisite course or class, or for the grade level preceding the one we are teaching. If I am teaching second grade reading, it is important for me to know the phonemes that were mastered in first grade and which ones were only introduced. If I am teaching an Algebra II class, I will want to know what concepts were mastered in Algebra I. Before we begin presenting this year's learning objectives, it would be wise to review briefly last year's objectives with our students. This will help us to build on a solid foundation and insure that what we teach actually sticks. If we just start building without insuring the foundation, then all of our hard work putting up walls may be in vain and the faulty foundation will not be able to hold them up. Most curriculums build in this review, but if yours does not, then the time and effort you put into this process will certainly pay off. In addition, for most of our students, there has been a lapse of time between the previous course or year and ours therefore a little review time is always beneficial. Though we might be thinking that it is not our responsibility nor do we have the time for this review, investing in the foundation our students have will help us to build structures that will not crumble. It will prevent us from having to go back again and again to re-teach principles that our students just do not have the prerequisite knowledge for.

Hoping we are all convinced, let's move to the next step which will be to write our scope and sequence for the course or class that we will be teaching. First list the title of the course (Second Grade History, Fifth grade math, British Literature 3101, etc.), the date or year we will teach it in (Fall 2020, etc.) and the publishing information of the text which will be used. We can add to this our contact and conference information and even hand this guide out to our parents so they have a copy of our road map.

Most curriculums provide us with a scope and sequence; we take this and divide it into quarters, six week periods, semesters or whatever time frame we are working within. This will give us a general idea of what our target is for each period. We will write the concepts in terms of learning objectives, which simply put means that we write the outcomes or end results. For examples, "The student will know and use subjective and objective pronouns correctly, or the student will know and understand the events leading to the Civil War, etc. This part of annual planning, gives us vital information: it tells us what and when our students will learn vital concepts. It also helps us to focus on the concepts that are crucial for the next year's success. Without this helpful tool and this annual planning, we sometimes get as far as we can in our text, but leave out some very crucial objectives which our students will need to succeed in the next class. We could also find ourselves majoring on minor objectives and never getting to the really important ones.

Once we have divided our objectives or learning outcomes into periods, we will then break them down into weeks. Knowing what we will need to teach each week will save us a lot of time when we do our weekly planning. We will know exactly what is taught in each week; this will make it easy to know what to teach each day. It also helps us to see the detailed picture of our year, and becomes our "game schedule".

There are many names for this guide that we are preparing; course syllabus, teaching objectives, scope and sequence, course overview, etc.; I like to call this plan our curriculum guide, our guide to presenting the curriculum which we are using. A curriculum guide is similar to the course syllabi that college professors prepare and hand out to their students. It is a sort of teaching objectives goal sheet. It is a vital tool for effective teaching because we need to know where we are going before we depart. It is our trip planning road map which helps us reach our destination. It is a listing of those very essential goals which we cannot reach unless we write them down. As in playing basketball or shooting targets, we could not score any points or shoot the bull's eye if there were no goal nets or if we could not see the target. The curriculum guide that we prepare annually helps us to have a clear target to shoot for. It also gives us our game schedule so that we are prepared for each game. For example, our guide tells us that in the third week of a high school English class that our students will learn the components of writing a five paragraph essay, and that by the ninth week they will have mastered this skill.

We will add to the section of objectives of our curriculum guide a section entitled, evaluation or assessment in which we will note the grading scale, the weight of each grade type and the schedule for evaluation. For example, the grading scale for a high school course might be 70 to 100 with 70 being the first passing mark and 100 the maximum number of points. We might note that either a quiz or test will be administered each week, and that tests will be weighted 64% while quiz/hw/other grades will count 36%. We would also add to this section any major projects which would be graded, for example a research paper valued as a test grade or an end of period fitness test with its value. Here we might also describe our testing or assessment format; First grade phonics tests will include a written exam and an oral exam with each part weighing 50%. A notation may be made here regarding how we will assess the final outcomes of a college course; i.e. in order to pass oral communications, the student will effectively respond to an extemporaneously given question. Etc.

This "Curriculum Guide" which consists of course information, learning outcomes, and assessment information, becomes a "living" document when we use it weekly, when we add to it as we teach, and when we review it at the end of the year or semester. For this purpose, title the last section "Comments". It is very effective to make notes in red on effective techniques, unusually challenging concepts, interesting web sites we visited, field trips we took with contact information on each one of them, that interesting lab experiment that made the concept real to our students, etc... Before beginning the next year, review the guide and the notations you made and make the most important ones a permanent part of the guide for next year. And when we get promoted to teach something else, we can leave this important "living" document to the teacher who will replace us, and he or she will benefit from our experience instead of having to re-invent everything. Ultimately, the students in our school that we may never teach will benefit from our experience and from the way that we left this "living document" even when we are no longer in the school or teaching that particular class. Samples for you to use as guides will be found in the appendix. Most accrediting organizations require these documents anyway, and someone usually writes them, but too often, they are filed in a binder for the benefit of the site visit team and never used by the teacher. It is important for you as a teacher to understand the value of them, write them, refer to them weekly to track the progress of your class, make notations, and review them annually. Actually using them (wisdom) is a beneficial, essential teaching tool. (Sample #'s 1-3)

WEEKLY PLANNING

Once we have the plan for the entire year and have pinpointed the skills with which our students should enter our class or course, then we must take some time weekly to plan our detailed learning adventures. The first part of weekly planning is writing the Weekly Lesson Plan. 'We begin by knowing our objectives for the quarter, or semester, which we have already broken down by weeks. Now it is just a matter of dividing those weekly outcomes into daily objectives. Our weekly lesson plans should include the time, day and location of our class; the concept to be taught each day; the pages of the material to be covered or read independently by the students; the student assignments (homework); and any additional items or equipment that might be necessary for each class (projector, cow eyes for dissection, baking soda for a demonstration, basketball for game etc...) Color coding these items helps them stand out; for example, items we need to obtain before class in red; learning objectives highlighted in yellow and homework in blue. We can also plan and note those six steps to "really teaching" that we will learn in a later chapter.

The task of preparing weekly lesson plans for an elementary class or for five subjects in a secondary or post-secondary class should not take more than about one hour. Most teachers at the pre-school, elementary, and secondary levels are required to submit weekly lesson plans to their supervisors. When I was a school principal, it was always difficult to get teachers to submit these lesson plans on time... It seemed that many teachers disliked this weekly task. I believe that having an understanding of the value of writing out the weekly road map and the tools needed to accomplish our goals help us to value this vital tool. The weekly lesson plan book/notebook for teachers is like the agenda or calendar for other professionals. Not only does it contain the vital information on what and when objectives will be taught and assessed, it should contain all appointments, duty schedules, parent contact information, and could even contain notes on student and parent communications. We should keep it with us both at school and at home. (Sample #4)

Let us talk about how we actually write these plans. First, pull your "Curriculum Guide" and the books you will teach from (PK-High School), and your notes and files for post-secondary. The guide will help us to see what needs to be covered during this week of instruction whether we meet daily or once or twice a week. We take into consideration the pace of our students, and the learning objectives we are trying to reach in this quarter, semester etc..., and looking at the end result we write down the objectives, pages, activities etc... which we will have to reach to get us there. This is the time to seek to add variety to our class presentation (we will deal with teaching styles in a later chapter), and to add variety to our student involvement. If your norm for teaching is lecture, consciously make decisions to have the students learn a concept inductively this week. This is also the time when you will consider a field trip or a virtual field trip through the internet or a special demonstration or even guest speaker. (Remember to note these on the "Living Curriculum Guide" for future use.) This is the time to be creative! Do the same thing for each different course or subject that you will teach. Again, this should not take much time. We are not studying our material here, we are just putting together the plan for the week.

The second part of weekly planning is actually studying the material that we are going to teach. Not too much study needs to go into introducing addition of one digit numbers with first graders so your task as lower elementary teachers will be to find ways to present the material so that students grasp it. In these grades, this signifies looking for the most interesting, student active teaching techniques so that our teaching is both memorable and clear. For those who teach at higher levels, this is the time to read the material, simplify it by putting it into outline format, or step by step format for math classes and even prepare our power-point or overhead slides. We prepare in this way instead of just teaching straight from the text in order to pull out and simplify the most important concepts or material. These notes are also invaluable if a student happens to be absent for a few days, and for those exceptional students who have difficulty taking notes in class. Regardless of our expertise in our field of teaching, we should still study to show ourselves approved, teachers who will not be embarrassed or ashamed if our leader happens to join us for class (II Tim.2:15).

Here, I would like to pause to discuss the danger of over studying or understudying. Some of us, especially those who are just entering the teaching vocation, study so much and prepare even to the degree of rehearsing every sentence in front of a mirror. This over-preparation stems from our desire to do our very best, but in many cases makes us slaves to our notes and thus rigid and mechanical. This creates a tense atmosphere which does not allow for our students' needs to be met. If we study our material adequately and apply some of the skills which will be presented in this book, we can relax and rest on the fact that we are called to this vocation and therefore have everything in us to succeed at it.

When we do not prepare, and this happens to the best of us, then obviously we will have to "fake it till we make it", but this cannot be our norm of operating. Some of us are fortunate to have a personality type that is very entertaining and naturally attracts our students' attention. We love to be with our students and they with us, and thus our gifts of "talk" and "performance" could lead us to the idea that preparation is not necessary. Unfortunately, sooner or later, our students will realize that they are not learning everything they should be learning in spite of the fact that they are having a lot of fun, and since we teachers truly desire to teach, we will fail. In addition, some of us love our subject matter so much, and have spent a lot of time becoming experts in our fields, and therefore do not see the need to study much. Though we know our material, we must still study and prepare to help make what is so exciting and interesting and simple to us, exciting and interesting and simple to our students. All of us, regardless of personality type, expertise in our field of instruction or years of teaching experience need to take the time to prepare. Whichever category we are in, let's take note because our purpose is to be effective teachers, and to accomplish this, we must both know our subject matter and be able to present it in such a way that our students learn, understand, and apply it.

I strongly recommend that our weekly study time result in written, typed, or power point outlines of what we will be teaching. These notes should be organized by topics and pages covered and should be numbered so that we can easily reference them. If it is the first time teaching a particular course or grade, then this study and documentation will take some time. Having well written outlines organized by topics and pages taught will save so much time next year, and again, these outlines can be passed on to the teacher who takes your classes when you are promoted. Even if it is the tenth time we have taught this course, and we already have our outlines written or typed, we should still review our notes looking for more dynamic methods of presenting the material or adding the most current information to them.

We must not allow ourselves to just take the text book and teach straight from it, or have the students teach themselves by reading the text book out loud or silently at home or in class. If this were all that was necessary for students to learn, and for some students it is, then teachers would not be necessary, we could just issue the text book and have them instruct themselves. Even though we know our material well, our notes are our guide as we KIS (keep it simple), teach the essentials, and break down the material.

KNOWLEDGE AND UNDERSTANDING ARE PRE-REQUISITES OF COGNITIVE THINKING

Let's take some time here to add another philosophical foundation to help us teach so that students actually learn. We teachers are guides and facilitators; we show our students how. Of course, we do want to master the art of teaching students to think and reason for themselves, but in order for them to think at higher levels, we must first impart knowledge and guide them to understand this knowledge. Then our students can use this knowledge and understanding to apply what they have learned; to reason; to deduct; to think critically. This is what I have referred to as "wisdom". Therefore, let's add this basic component to our teaching philosophy: teachers take difficult material and maybe material that is uninteresting to our students, and make it simple, interesting, and relevant to them. (i.e. Teach the body systems in anatomy in a logical organized way so that students can keep the information we give them. Use teaching techniques that help them understand each system and how it relates to all of the others. Then use their understanding of this information to aid them in taking care of their own bodies). We take concepts that are large and complex and break them down into smaller simpler parts so that our students can see how each part relates to the whole. (For example, take each battle of a particular war and lead to the outcome of that war and the impact which that war had on the culture, how it could have been prevented, and how we can use this understanding today).

We should also take something that is very complicated and make it simple by breaking it down into smaller steps: determine how many square feet of cement will be necessary to lay the foundation of a building with various shapes by pointing out that there are semi-circles and squares and triangles in the plan and reviewing the formulas for the areas of each. We should take a lot of information and narrow it down to what is really the vital information (teach students the foreign language vocabulary they will need to order in a restaurant, or get to the airport, find a restroom instead of asking them to memorize lists and lists of words). We must take what is foreign and make it familiar for our students (Teach, review and drill the vowel and consonant graphemes with their phonemes until they are familiar; then put those together to read syllables, then words, then sentences).

HUMILITY: COMING DOWN TO THE LEVEL OF OUR STUDENTS

Teachers, no matter how many degrees or years of experience we have, must also be humble and not high minded. We must have the mind and humility of Christ, that being God Himself did not think anything of becoming a man, or coming down to our level. We in turn, with our many or few years of experience or much or little expertise must also seek to come down to the level of our students. As a part of our weekly study, let's make it our responsibility to endeavor to make it simple. I have found that sometimes teachers who were not the best in a particular subject make the best teachers of that subject because first, they empathize with the students who do not grasp the concept quickly. Second, knowing that every person is not a prodigy in a particular field, they make an effort to make it simple, and thus all of their students learn. It is easy to teach the geniuses, but the real challenge is reaching all of our students. If my most challenged student understands, then I know that all of my students understand and can apply what they have learned. Here again, I must emphasize that belief that it is my responsibility (to the degree of the level of my students, see chapter 1) to teach them, and if they did not learn, then I did not teach.

PREPARING TO TEACH MATH

Here is a paragraph dedicated to all of the wonderful math teachers. Why are you so special? Because when we take a survey of students, the majority of them will say that Math is their worst subject. Math is one of those get it or sink classes in school, and if you did not get it from the beginning, it will haunt you for the rest of your math classes and even for the rest of your life. It is also one of the classes that so many students struggle with. Math is not hard, but it takes a special guide and some teaching skills to "really teach" math. For those of you who do not teach math, do not skip this paragraph, as it will help no matter what you teach. I must say that I am not an expert in math, but I have taught many secondary and elementary math classes, and two things usually happen: first, the students ask me to be their permanent teacher, and second, ninety-nine per cent of the students pass. The first key is "MIS" and "KIS"(make it simple and keep it simple). The second is to teach math both digitally (actually working the problems for the students, showing my numerical work) and verbally (actually writing out the words as I speak them). To "MIS" and "KIS", we take that complicated book explanation and break it down into simple steps. I even make notations on my outline: step one, step two, step three, etc.... I will use a difficult homework problem as my example (usually the book explains with a simple illustration, then gives much more difficult problems for homework). I not only show every single step numerically, but I also explain verbally and write those words next to each step. A caution here. Since most math teachers are brilliant mathematicians, they have a tendency to skip steps assuming that students can follow and they therefore generally loose students.

We must show every step! Since I have first broken the concept down from large to small, or complicated to simple. I then demonstrated, told, and wrote each step, and required that my students took notes. These wonderful notes are like taking the teacher home with them. Third, I allowed them to do a few problems as I guided them through each step. And I do mean "them", as so many times teachers do all of the work or work the problems themselves instead of allowing the students to work the problem (including calculations) as the teacher guides them through the steps. Finally when it was time for them to do the problems (wisdom) independently, they could either perform them effectively, or if necessary, refer back to the notes which are both digital and verbal to guide them through the steps. Though we will discuss effective teaching techniques in a later chapter, right now we want to focus on preparing our weekly teaching outlines, and in math if these outlines "MIS" and "KIS" and note the numerical problems and verbal and written steps, our students will get it! How exciting is that!

To every teacher I would say, we all need to prepare on a weekly basis the material we expect our students to learn. Let us remind ourselves here that learning includes three steps: the acquisition of knowledge, the gaining of understanding, and the ability to apply the two (wisdom). Our preparation may take some time the first time that we teach a course, but if we have prepared and organized our outlines well, in subsequent years or semesters, our task of weekly preparation will be less laborious. Nevertheless, this preparation is necessary as we endeavor to enhance and enrich what we teach. When we prepare weekly, breaking the concepts down and making them simple, we position ourselves to become those excellent teachers we desire to be. We also enable our students to succeed not only in acquiring and understanding information, but in obtaining wisdom – the ability to apply what they have learned.

DAILY PREPARATION

Now we are ready for the last part of preparation, and by this time, you may be thinking, "Wow, stop, I do not have this much time to prepare!" Be encouraged, daily preparation does not take long, and it is the most exciting type of preparation. It takes a few minutes daily before you begin to teach, to prepare for the students, parents, and even colleagues that you will work with that day. I leave our discussion of daily planning for last, because it is in my opinion the most important, and I want it to stay in your minds.

Daily planning means reflecting on your students and believing and hoping for breakthroughs with them. It means seeking the wisdom to communicate effectively with that concerned parent in order to partner with them for the benefit of their child. It means thinking good thoughts about each student, and meditating on ways to present your material in a dynamic, interesting, and easy to understand way. It means maybe walking by each desk and just believing for the best for each student. It means walking through the classroom and seeing a peaceful but vibrant class. So many times we rush into the classroom and dive into the tasks of the day, but I encourage you to stop for a few minutes (5-10) to do some of these things before you begin your day. These few minutes invested in daily preparation will save many hours in parent conferences, in re-teaching lessons, and in frustration and aggravation.

INSPIRATION FROM THE MASTER TEACHER

Did you know that we have access to the greatest teacher that has ever lived on the earth? Yes, and this access is available to us twenty-four hours a day and seven days a week. This "Master Teacher" understands the needs and learning styles of each one of our students, and the most effective teaching techniques for each one of them. This "Master Teacher" is filled with the wisdom that we do not possess.

I would like to share one favorite example of this "Master Teacher" in my life. He was my rescuer the first year I taught a combination fifth and sixth grade class. I had replaced another teacher in November and therefore I did not have the advantage of learning all of the concepts they had already learned at the beginning of the year. I was certified to teach bilingual elementary education, but I had been out of the classroom for some time. The curriculum in this school was quite advanced, especially in math. I had no choice but to rely on the Holy Spirit to lead me and guide me and to show me things that I did not know. Though I did prepare, no amount of preparation could have made up for my lack of knowledge in some of the subjects, and for my inexperience with teaching this particular age group. In addition to that, I had five very "exceptional" students who I had no idea how to reach or teach. I can honestly say that because of the help of the "Master Teacher", to this day that was my most effective, exciting, and rewarding teaching year.

After many years of teaching, I have learned that during this difficult year of teaching, some of the techniques that I had used but had not been formally trained in, are actually pedagogically sound and taught in Master Degree programs in special education. And to think, all of this wisdom was made available to me during my daily preparation time as I asked the Holy Spirit to show me what to do with these students and how to best get the information across to my students so they could learn, understand and apply it later. Of course, this Guide does not just speak to us in our preparation time, but can be consulted even in the middle of a lesson when our students either have those blank looks of "I don't get it, or of I don't really care". This inspiration and even instruction received during daily preparation has proven to be the absolute most valuable teaching tool I have found. I recommend that each and every day, a few minutes be spent seeking wisdom from Him who inspires us and gives us knowledge of creative ideas.

DAILY PLANNING THROUGH INTERCESSION

Praying for our day and our students will also yield outstanding results. This can be done on our way to school or while we are making breakfast or showering. Taping a class roster on the inside of your medicine cabinet door will remind you to intercede for your classes as a group or for your students individually. We must take advantage of prayer, the change instigator, as an invaluable teaching technique. And when you pray, keep a pen and pad handy to write down ideas or even things that the Holy Spirit will give you to do, like bring an extra lunch to share with a student, or call a particular parent, or speak to a student about why they are so sleepy in class etc... You will have such an advantage!

DAILY PLANNING THROUGH POSITIVE CONFESSION

In addition to prayer, as a part of our daily planning, I also highly recommend saying out loud what we want to see in our students. This we can refer to as positive confessions, and if these statements come from the Bible, as you say them out loud, you will begin to believe them and then you will begin to see your students this way, and soon what you believe about your students will actually come to pass. (Sample # 5)

CLOSE THE DOOR WHEN YOU LEAVE THE HOUSE

Another part of daily preparation is learning to close the door when you leave your house. I mean that whatever is happening at home needs to stay in the house when you leave to teach. Entering the classroom should be like going on a trip. We forget about the house, the job, finances, problems etc. It is important not to take your school work home and also not to take your homework to school. So many teachers prefer to grade papers from home and prepare at home, and soon, it is difficult to distinguish between home and school. I recommend that you either arrive a little earlier or leave a little later, but leave school at school and home at home. Do all of your school work at school, and focus only on school while at school. When we focus our camera, it brings the image closer and clearer. The same happens with everything that we focus on. When we are at school, let us focus on school, and when at home, let us focus on our families. This will make us so much more effective in both places, and will alleviate much resentment from our families. It will also help us to be professional at school as we do not allow our personal challenges to affect our effectiveness in the classroom.

TO SUMMARIZE

I hope that this chapter on preparing to teach will be of much value to you. As we prepare to teach, we are planning to succeed, and because we are great teachers, not merely good ones, we desire to be effective. After all, if our students do not learn, then have we really taught? The most important and probably easiest form of preparation consists of our daily quest for guidance, inspiration and creativity from the Holy Spirit. Daily planning can also include praying to change situations, and speaking and believing what we want to see in our students. In addition to daily preparation, we must prepare to teach on a weekly basis by writing lesson plans (our itinerary for learning experiences), and by writing or typing our notes and outlines for the subject matter we will teach. We remind ourselves that it is our job to MIS and KIS (make it simple and keep it simple). Finally, preparation includes annual preparation; the review of where our students are when they enter our class, and the mapping of what they will learn and when they will learn it by completing that "living" curriculum guide. We will find that these three easy preparation steps (annual planning, weekly planning, and daily planning) will put us on the road to being "great", not just "good" teachers.

APPLICATION (WISDOM)

1. *Annual Preparation: Write a guide or scope and sequence for each class you will teach:*

   a. *Gather the scope & sequence or course syllabus for the pre-requisite course to the courses or grades you will teach this year. Make notations of the skills your students should have mastered. Put together a simple assessment to be administered before you begin teaching this year's objectives. Plan to review concepts which your students may not have mastered.*

   b. *Note the text books, publishers etc... of the books you will be using for each class.*

   c. *Get the scope and sequence for the course or grade you will be teaching and divide the objectives into semesters, quarters, weeks, or whatever time frame your course is divided into. Once written divide them again into the weeks in each time period.*

   d. *Note your grading scale and assessment criteria (Tests: 66%, Quiz/HW:34%)*

   e. *Note your form of evaluation or assessment (Weekly test or quiz; weekly oral comprehension check)*

    f. *Leave a space for comments (Students had difficulty with certain concept therefore three days were spent here instead of two; Visiting the flight museum reenforced the concept of aerodynamics; guest speaker contact information; etc.)*

2. *Weekly Preparation: Write a weekly lesson plan remembering to color code.*

3. *Weekly Preparation: Study and prepare your teaching notes for one class; each page of notes should include the title of the topic along with the text page numbers being covered and should also be paginated to keep them in order.*

4. *Daily Preparation: Try speaking the "Student Affirmations" out loud for one week and note the results.*

Chapter Four

DISCIPLINE – A MATTER OF AUTHORITY

Key Points

1. *Good classroom management stems from an understanding of and an implementation of the principles of being in and under authority. As we submit to those in authority over us, we gain the right to be in authority, and our students submit to our authority.*

2. *We should praise the students who do what is right and issue consequences to those who do wrong; thus those who do wrong should fear (healthily respect) us, and those who submit to our instruction should be blessed by us.*

3. *We teach our students to do right, not just out of fear, but so that they can have the peace of a clear conscience.*

4. *Be ready to correct and reward when it is convenient and when it is not; when we feel like it, and when we do not; be consistent.*

5. *Excellent classroom management requires training, rewards and consequences.*

6. *Use love and logic when disciplining; discipline in love showing empathy for the student's situation, and encourage students to logically determine and experience the consequences of their choices.*
7. *A prepared, interesting and dynamic teacher is a great deterrent of discipline problems.*
8. *We cannot teach our students if we cannot control them*

Thus far, we have discussed teaching as a vocation (an occupation that is based upon a certain "gifting" and "calling"), which enables us to impact the future, whose result requires learning (knowledge, understanding, and wisdom). We established that in order to truly teach our students, we would first have to gain their trust by establishing a relationship with them. Finally, we acknowledged the importance of annual, weekly and daily preparation in order to effectively teach. Now, let us move on to the topic of discipline, or what is also referred to as classroom management. I chose to discuss discipline before instruction methodology because no matter how great our teaching techniques might be, I strongly believe that if we cannot manage our students, then we cannot teach them! In this chapter, we will first lay some very important foundations or principles regarding discipline, the main one being: discipline is a "matter of authority". Then we will learn the importance of rewards and consequences in establishing an effective learning environment. We will discuss the "love and logic" philosophy of discipline and finally review some key behavior problem deterrents; preparation, organization and time management, and dynamic teaching.

DISCIPLINE, A MATTER OF AUTHORITY

Having good discipline is a matter of knowing, understanding, and operating in authority; thus my statement: "Discipline is a matter of authority." We will begin with a discussion of the term discipline and the foundational components of it. It is interesting that the word "discipline" is almost taboo in today's educational arena. Our cultural aversion to this word has lead us to exchange it for a term that is more palatable and acceptable in the current educational arena, namely, "classroom management." Along the same line, another word that is generally met with resistance, especially in the United States, is "authority". Could a cause of this be our independent and democratic spirit which causes us and our students to resist being told what and when to do anything? Whatever the reason, there is little doubt that both terms – "discipline" and "authority" -seem to have connotations of rigidness and control and even antiquation in education and in society in general. Yet because the correct understanding of these two words is critical to your success as a teacher, I would like to define both and even be able to use each without the risk of having some readers discard the chapter entirely because of the feelings these two words might draw out.

Please do not get the wrong impression. Though I believe strongly in discipline and know that understanding and operating in and under authority is the key to attaining classroom management that produces a productive learning environment, let me take the time to stress again the need for establishing a good relationship with our students... If we do not first gain the trust and establish a good relationship with our students, we will never gain their respect for our authority, nor their succession to us of the management of the class. Nevertheless, I also want to stress another important point: if we cannot discipline our students, then we cannot teach them.

DISCIPLINE

Let us first define the word discipline. According to Webster, it is the treatment suited to a disciple, a learner. How interesting that discipline and disciple (learner) come from the same root word, and that discipline is that treatment suited to a learner. In other words, every learner needs discipline in order to be a learner. Another definition for discipline is the development of faculties (learning) by instruction, exercise, and training. Therefore I believe that a very excellent definition of discipline is developing our students by teaching them (instruction), by providing them with opportunities to apply what they learn (exercise), and by taking them through these practices over and over until they have become internalized and have become second nature to our students (training).

Is it becoming clearer that we cannot educate without the use of discipline? A further exploration of the true meaning of "discipline" opens even greater understandings of its importance. C.J. Smith states that discipline is "the removal of bad habits and substitution of good." There is little doubt then that to substitute "good" would mean that discipline is going to be very beneficial to our students.

Webster offers additional definitions for the word discipline: to accustom to an action; to bring under control; to teach subordination; to form a habit of obedience; to drill; to train. I hope that you are gathering from these meanings that discipline is a good thing and the treatment that every learner actually needs in order to learn. Would you also agree that it is better to be a disciplined person or student rather than an undisciplined one? Would we rather hire a disciplined contractor, teacher, dentist, doctor, housekeeper over an undisciplined one who lacks training or is unaccustomed to appropriate actions, or does not have the necessary skills under their control,? Certainly being disciplined seems to demonstrate excellence, diligence, punctuality, and accomplishments. As educators and parents, is it not our desire to help to train individuals who because of discipline are able to really impact our world in a positive way?

FROM EXTERNALLY DISCIPLINED TO SELF-DISCIPLINED

Our goal as educators will be to help our students become self-disciplined both in their behavior at school and in their work ethic. We must first show our students what we expect of them. Next, we must give them opportunities to practice what we expect as we guide them. Then they will exhibit he taught and practiced behaviors independently and without our external influence. We must instruct, then train, and then coach our students.

As instructors, we show our students the behavior or classroom procedure that we expect. Then we explain why this behavior is beneficial. Finally we teach them how to accomplish this behavior. We then become their trainers, taking them through and actually modeling the exercises of behaving in the way that we have just taught them. At this juncture, we will need to reward excellent behavior, give consequences for negative behavior, and re-walk our students through the desired behavior until it becomes their own behavior. This is the stage where we require the behavior that we have taught. Finally, as coaches and from the side lines, we call in the learned and much practiced "plays". We make adjustments during time-outs and even in after game meetings. We may have to re-teach or practice some of the plays again if on game day we do not get the desired results, but eventually our students learn the plays and execute them independently without the need for rewards or consequences.

The Ezzo's, authors of <u>Training Kids God's Way</u>, make an analogy of this training with a warehouse. As teachers, we place cans on the shelves of our students' "warehouses"- cans of honor, respect, diligence, obedience, concern for others etc... If these "cans" have been placed there, when the student comes to a situation where one of these cans is needed, he will know what he is to do. If there is no "can" stored in his "warehouse" for a particular situation, then he will not know how to respond or may respond in an undesirable way. Because we have taught them what to do when the teacher is talking, or while working with their project group, or when someone is bothering them, or when they have finished the current assignment, we can count on them behaving in the way that we have taught them, and our classes (university, high school or elementary) can enjoy that optimum learning environment. If our students have the proper teaching or "cans", and they choose to do the opposite, because they have been taught, their conscience will bother them until they do what is right. Without the proper "cans", there is no possibility of remorse for behaving in a way that might feel good to the student, but which is detrimental to the well-being of the entire group.

Now, let us discuss some specific classroom management goals and then examine our roles as instructors, trainers, and finally as coaches. Regarding discipline and even instruction, it is first very important to teach our students what we expect of them. Our expectations don't have to be elaborate and we don't need fifty rules written on the wall of our classroom. In my personal teaching experience, I always had three very simple rules, whether I was teaching first grade or adults. The first was not to speak while someone else was speaking and to get permission to speak before speaking. The second was not to move about without permission. The final was to work diligently. I found that these three rules of classroom discipline covered everything.

Students respected me as their teacher and other students who were speaking by adding to or questioning only when given my say-so. They moved about the room with my consent or under clearly established guidelines to protect the safety and concentration of everyone in the classroom. Can you imagine all fifty college students up and about at the same time or all twenty five kindergarten students in random movement with scissors and glue in hand? We can be sure that little learning will be accomplished when this behavior prevails. Finally working diligently meant that they were engaged either in the discussion or in their seatwork or on their project, etc. Let us assume that these three behaviors are the goals for our students, be they elementary, high school, or adult learners. How then do we reach the ultimate goal of these behaviors being their actual nature?

INSTRUCTORS, TRAINERS, AND COACHES GUIDING STUDENTS IN BECOMING SELF-DISCIPLINED

We can reach the goal of self-disciplined students in three stages, as we function in three roles; instructor, trainer, and coach. As an instructor, I want to first teach my students my three expectations. I parallel this stage with stocking the shelves of my students' warehouses with beneficial expectations. These simple expectations and instructions could be posted in the classroom for younger students, or just verbally expressed to older students, but my ultimate goal is that they be stocked internally in the hearts and minds of my students so that they will act them out even when I am not near.

Teaching our students why these expectations are necessary is as vital as having clearly communicated expectations. Why not speak out any time they want to like they were able to at home with only three other siblings and their parents to compete with? Well let's have them imagine or even practice having everyone express their need or idea at once. Could anyone hear anyone else? Could the teacher meet their need or even hear it? Could anyone hear the instruction? Could anyone concentrate? Probably not, and the children will get to experience that when we are in large group settings, it is important to get permission to speak, and to be careful not to speak when someone else is speaking. Since after one or two presentations most people do not internalize what was taught or told, in our role as instructors we may have to go over this expected behavior and the reason for it a few times or even many times. This may test our patience, but it is extremely important to persist until the desired behavior and the reason for it is clearly understood.

In the next stage, as we move from instructors to trainers, it will be our responsibility to take our students through the drill or have our students practice the expected behavior over and over until it becomes as second nature to them, or until they internalize it. We will use my second expectation to discuss our "trainer" role. Our expected outcome is that my students, for their own safety and well-being and that of the other members of the class, stay in their seats unless given permission to do otherwise. Here, we will use first graders as our teaching group as this expectation has usually become "second nature" to our adult students, but is very difficult for our younger students. I have already taught them the "what and why", and given them instructions on raising their hand in order to leave their seats. (One finger to go to the restroom; two for a drink; three to get something from their bag; ten for an emergency; and five for everything else.) Now, I want to run them through the drill until this behavior becomes ingrained in their thinking, because naturally, up to this point, they never had to ask for permission to move about their house or backyard; this school life is so different from home life! I actually have them practice raising one finger when they need to go to the bathroom, and all ten for the emergency of "I need to throw up", or "My heart is hurting", or "My neighbor hurt himself." We have great fun practicing this behavior and the other two. We go over and over and over the "plays" (speak with permission, leave your seat with permission, and work diligently) until we feel that everyone gets it, and now we are ready for the big game, and trainers now become coaches!

Today we start our reading circles, and while we give all of our attention to these small groups of six or seven, we want the rest of the students to follow our three rules. We know they can do it, we have trained and trained, but within the first five minutes of the first reading circle, oh no! We have talkers, and wanderers, and even slackers! Oh my! Do not worry, do not be dismayed, put on your coaching hat, call a time out, and remind everyone of the game plan. Then go back to your circle, and all will be perfect? I do not think so, but as coach, I may have to call that "wanderer to the huddle" and re-explain the play, and even sit him on the bench as a consequence to that behavior. I will also want to reward verbally or otherwise that table of students who is working so diligently. As a coach, I must remember that even though we have practiced the plays over and over and I have told them over and over what and why I expect what I expect, it will always take time and rewards and consequences to reach that ultimate goal of self-discipline. This is true of all levels of students – even at the university level. The reward for upper level students can be reduced homework, skipping a test, dropping the lowest grade, etc. Some will reach the goals faster than others, but I believe that ultimately every one of my students will reach those goals.

To conclude this part of our discussion on discipline, I want to refer to Proverbs 22:6 and note an important command and promise. Here it says that if we train up a child or a student in the way they should go, that when he is older or mature or fully grown, he will not depart from this way. Obviously, it is best to do this training when individuals are chronologically younger, as they are much more pliable and moldable, but even if we must begin this training with high school students or even adult learners, when they are mature, they will not depart from the way we have trained them. I want to encourage those who teach young adults or older adults. Sometimes they are in our classes, and they have not learned to be diligent. We may be tempted to give up on them because by this stage of their lives they should have already learned this discipline. Though this is true, the fact is that some have not achieved the necessary inner control or restraint, and as their teacher (instructor, trainer, and coach), I can make a difference. You know the saying that you cannot teach an old dog new tricks? Well I do not believe it. Maybe it is harder to train an adult than a younger person, but all humans are created with the ability to learn no matter how old they are. The key to accomplishing this very necessary task is helping the undisciplined person to develop the desire to learn and to change, and then I believe we can influence their lives and enable them to be all that they were created to be!

At this point, with the foundations of the benefits of and the how to obtain discipline laid, let us now move on to the concept of authority, and how discipline is so much a matter of how both we and our students understand it.

AUTHORITY

Authority is defined as rightful power; the right to command by virtue of office or position; the power derived from respect or esteem. Rightful power — authority is power that rightfully belongs to those who are in authority. We as teachers, as well as parents, police officers, governing authorities, etc... all have legitimate power and the right to command or control by virtue of the positions which we hold. I repeat, teachers, as well as parents, police officers, governing authorities, etc... all have rightful power and the right to command others by virtue of the positions which we hold. Where does this legitimate power come from? According to this Webster definition, this power to command is derived from the very office or position we hold or also through respect or esteem.

Certain offices or positions should naturally command respect. For example, the President by virtue of his position commands our respect and honor. Likewise, so do parents, persons in civil positions such as police officers, and yes, teachers. In most of the nations of the world, a teacher is held in high esteem and respected accordingly. Regretfully, it is only recently that the position of teacher in the United States has been held with decreasing respect and honor.

In addition, respect and honor (authority) are also derived or gained or earned from respect or esteem granted to us by others. This is where establishing that trusting, loving relationship is important. Some students have been taught to respect a person because of their office or position; those who have not been taught this important principle say, "You must earn my respect." I say, let us both earn our students' respect, and also teach them about this respect due to others because of position.

The Bible describes this principle very clearly and completely in Romans 13:1. Basically it states that there is no authority (rightful power to command) except from God, and that the authorities that are were appointed by Him. Many, and especially in the United States, have difficulty with this concept, and it is important that we understand it well, before we can apply it and actually teach it to those of our students who may not know it. Some would say, you mean that corrupt President, or policeman, or that mean teacher, or even abusive parent was placed in authority by God? According to Romans 13, the answer is yes. What about us teachers? Are we placed in these positions by God? If we believe Romans 13, the answer is still, yes. So if this is true, and we know that it is, then we have been placed in positions of authority over our students by God Himself. This truth, or piece of knowledge, if we understand it correctly, and act on it, can make a major difference in how we see ourselves in our classrooms, and thus in how we operate in our classrooms.

The application of this understood knowledge (wisdom) is that we carry ourselves with a degree of confidence and strength that will command the respect of our students. Actually it is this understanding that we are in charge and have a right to be in charge that will help us maintain the discipline in our classrooms that is necessary if we are to truly teach our students.

Having this knowledge and understanding and acting upon it will and should mean that we have the lawful right to be in control or in charge of our students, and to manage our classes accordingly. It will not and should not cause us to become dictators in our classrooms.

So in order for us not to abuse of this authority, the administration of it must be motivated by our love, concern, and commitment to our students. We want to guard ourselves from being abusive with this rightful power which has been commanded to us due to our positions, but we also want to demonstrate the fact that we are rightfully in authority.

When in staff development conferences and I am teaching the principle of God given authority to the position of a teacher, I like to bring along a crown and place it on the heads of the teachers attending the seminar. When we really understand our authority in the classroom, it is like wearing a ruler's crown. Of course, we want to act as a benevolent and kind ruler, but a ruler or person in authority nevertheless. Try this exercise at home by walking around the room envisioning yourself with a crown to remind you of your rightful power and position. I recommend this activity if you are feeling a little intimidated or unsure of yourself as a teacher or professor. This humble, yet confident, courageous, and bold attitude in front of our students and even their parents will help us gain that respect and honor, which is necessary if we are to teach our students. It will also help the parents of our students trust in us and therefore confidently support us as we teach their children. If we demonstrate confidence in ourselves, the parents of our students will be able to believe in us too. And now that we have established and clarified our rightful and honorable position as teachers, let us look at the important principle that we must teach our students regarding submitting to authority.

COMPLETE SUBMISSION, NOT NECESSARILY COMPLETE OBEDIENCE

Because certain authority figures have at times abused their power, many would advocate not honoring or respecting any authority figure, especially not without strong reservations or severe scrutiny. Some argue, "How can anyone be expected to respect and submit to these types of authorities?" In Romans 13:2, we find that we are expected to submit and not resist authorities over us. This scripture does not say we are only expected to submit to and obey authorities that we are in agreement with or that we like or that we have voted into office. We are required to submit completely to all who are in authority. Here again, some would strongly disagree with a teaching that we are to submit without question to those who are in authority, and because of much abuse of authority could say so rightfully. It is here that a critical difference needs to be presented, one that is not widely understood. It is the understanding that complete submission does not mean complete obedience.

God requires complete submission, not necessarily complete obedience. Let me explain. We can demonstrate submission to authority while not necessarily obeying every command. Let us look at some examples of this so that we can understand completely. Let us say that our school principal asks us to alter a record of one of our students to show a grade that he or she did not actually earn. Or let us say that we need to show more students in a special program in order to get additional funding, and we are asked by our principal to slightly alter those numbers. We can say to our principal, "Look, I respect your position, and would really like to help this student, or to get our school more funding, but I cannot do this as it would be dishonest." What if we are teaching our students to submit to authority figures, and there is a teacher or professor who is asking them to meet them after class at their home. We should teach the student to very respectfully decline obedience while continuing to honor their position of authority. I hope I am making this point clear – complete submission does not require blind obedience. We are allowed to disobey respectfully when we know that what we are being asked to do is not correct morally or ethically.

WILLING OBEDIENCE PRODUCES GREAT RESULTS

On the other hand, we do want to teach our students to willingly obey all those who are in authority over them when those commands are morally and ethically correct. There are numerous scriptures which deal with the blessings of obedience, but one of my favorites is found in Isaiah 1:19, which states that a willing attitude of obedience will result in us receiving the "good of the land" or the best there is. I would like to emphasize here the importance of willing obedience. According to Webster, to be willing means to be favorably disposed or ready; to be prompt to act or respond; to accept by choice and without reluctance. To obey means to follow the commands of or to comply. Therefore, if we can train (discipline) our students to choose to comply with our commands readily and promptly, then we can insure them blessings both from us and in life in general. Since we want them to be blessed in life, we also want to teach and train them in the principle of willing obedience.

You might ask, "How can you train or teach a willing attitude; an inward position that is reflected in one's actions. Because willingness is an inward position, we must help our students to desire to obey because of the rewards of obedience.

You might be thinking that this is bribery; no, just motivation. As we reward their obedience, they become conditioned or trained to obey willingly and promptly because they know that rewards or blessings follow obedience. In a short time, willing, prompt and complete obedience will become a part of their "discipline" or learned behavior, and will produce a positive learning environment. Now that we have discussed obedience and its place in authority, let us continue with our discussion on the topic of authority and submission to it. Our goal is to be able to follow this principle of authority accurately, teach it to our students, and thus reap the benefits of submission to authority. For that purpose, let us return to Romans 13:2 to discuss the consequences of not submitting to authority.

The basic concept is that if we resist the authorities that have been placed over us, then we resist the One who placed them in those positions, and this will bring a negative judgment on whoever is resisting. What does it mean to resist? Simply, it means to go against, to push against, or to be uncooperative with. Unfortunately, due to the lack of knowledge, understanding, and wisdom, many people do resist those in positions of authority. The results are problems for these individuals, not for the person in authority. That is why it is essential and crucial that we understand this foundational principle and teach it to our students. A great motivational understanding for the reluctant student would be to teach them that the wise person who has learned to respect and honor those who are in authority will always find much favor in life. Consider this. As a teacher, which student has more favor with you, the one who respects and does what you ask, or the one who does what he pleases when he pleases; the one who answers with yes, Sir or no Ma'am, or the one who just grunts or says yeah, or just defies your request? Many think that this type of respect is old fashioned, but to date, I have always received favorable treatment from my parents, my teachers, a police officer or any other person in authority when I have respected them and responded with a yes Sir, or no Sir.

RESPECTFUL AND SUBMISSIVE TEACHERS PRODUCE RESPECTFUL AND SUBMISSIVE STUDENTS

I am spending time with this foundational principle of authority both for us to learn and use in our own lives, and also so that we are equipped to share it with our students who may have never understood this principle. Remember in a previous chapter when we talked about our students when fully trained would become like their teacher? This holds true with regards to respect for authority and for being disciplined. If you respect the authorities which are over you as a teacher (principal, parents of your students, government officials, etc...), the students will observe this, and then not only learn to do the same, but they will also offer you that same honor. If your mode of operandi is to do your own thing and talk about the principal in a negative way, then your students will do the same with you.

Over the many years that I have trained and supervised teachers and worked with them regarding classroom management and discipline, I have found two reasons why a teacher has difficulty with classroom management. The first, which is easily curable, is that they do not know what to do or how to do it. The second, not so easily remedied, is that they themselves have not learned to respect authority and are undisciplined themselves. In the later part of this chapter, we will discuss in detail the and how of maintaining good discipline.

For now, we must learn the very beneficial principle of making a decision to submit to our authorities so that our students will in turn submit to us. Let us also remember that wisdom is actually applying this newly understood principle.

UNDER AUTHORITY AND IN AUTHORITY

Now that we are in agreement that we must be under authority in order for our students to grant us the authority (power, command) over them in the classroom, we must also learn to walk in authority. Since there is no authority except from God, then He must have placed us in charge or in command over our students. Even though some would cringe at the thought of someone actually expecting students to submit to their teachers, this is what is necessary if we are going to create an environment of order in our classrooms; the environment that is good soil for learning. Much of their submission to our authority because of our position as teacher rests on us truly understanding and acting upon the knowledge that we are indeed in authority (in charge, with the power to carry out our authority). When we truly know and understand that we have rightful authority granted to us by God, because of our position, then we will act in a certain manner. Imagine a king, queen, or President. That crown, or that title, or that position causes them to act and even walk with a large degree of confidence, strength, and courage. When a teacher is not sure of himself or herself, students quickly detect weakness, and take full advantage of the situation. Therefore, it is important for us to carry ourselves both in action and words, with the assurance and confidence, which rightfully comes with the authority which has been given to us. This is why in staff development seminars for teachers, I brought a crown, and actually had those teachers who seem a little timid wear that crown to practice speaking with authority and confidence and moving with the demeanor of the rightful leader of the classroom.

I take a quick side note here to discuss the relationship between teacher and parent. Who has greater authority, teacher and school or parent? I believe that parents have primary and greater authority over their children than do teachers or the school. That God given authority is then shared with teachers and school when parents decide to send them to our schools. We must strive to partner with the parents of our students, so that our students are not confused or forced to choose between obeying and honoring their teacher instead of their parent, or vice versa. When parents and teachers can unite with a common goal and even common language, then nothing will be impossible for us to obtain as we train that student!

A TERROR NOT TO GOOD WORKS, BUT TO EVIL

As we discuss this important element of authority, let us go back to Romans thirteen and verse three, which states that rulers (people in positions of authority, i.e. parents, teachers, policemen) are not a terror to good works, but to evil. We should not be fearful to those students who are doing the right thing, but we should be a terror to those who are doing wrong. If we do not want to be afraid of those who are in authority over us, then all we have to do is do good, and according to this scripture we will receive praise from them.

Have you ever been racing down the freeway at fifteen miles over the speed limit when you see a police officer in your rear view mirror? What is your response? Terror! We even begin to pray that he did not notice how fast we were going and we vow never to speed again! On the other hand, you are driving down the freeway being very conscientious about staying within the speed limit and you see a police officer. Now what is your response? If you normally drive within the speed limit, your response will be one of no problem. Am I right? The same thing happens with us teachers and our principal. If we are doing what we are supposed to be doing, then it is not a problem for him or her to visit our classroom. The same thing happens with our students. If they obey us and do what they are supposed to be doing, then they will not fear us; though they will respect us. If they are doing wrong, they should fear us.

PRAISE THE "DO-GOODERS"

In verse four of Romans thirteen it says that those in authority are God's ministers toward us for good. In other words, figures, rules, and procedures of authority in our classrooms are there for the good of all of our students. The fact that we ask our students to get permission to speak just helps every student to be able to hear what is said. Discipline or classroom management helps us attain an environment which is conducive to learning for all of our students. It is good for our students, and when they do good, it is important for us to praise them. If we do, then those students who are doing what is right will not fear us.

Unfortunately, what can too often happen is that we express our wrath to the whole class, when there are usually only two or three doing "evil". This type of teacher behavior is generally counterproductive and lowers the morale of the class in general. Much more effective is praise and reward of those who are doing what is right. It is surprising to see how all of the other students (young or old) seek that word of encouragement or that blessing or that reward also. Praise and other rewards are excellent techniques for maintaining great classroom management!

EXECUTE WRATH ON THOSE THAT PRACTICE EVIL

In this same verse, it says that those who do evil should be afraid because we as people in authority are there to execute wrath on those who practice evil. This sounds very strong, so let me explain as I also re-emphasize the need to go back to chapter two and re-visit all of those skills necessary to establish a relationship of love and trust between ourselves and our students. If our students are doing wrong (talking when they should be working; teasing another student; writing on the desk; not doing their reading assignments; monopolizing the group discussion; sleeping during instruction, etc...) then they should fear us. If they do not, it is because we have not executed "wrath" on those who do evil. In other words, there has been no consequence for the negative or unwanted or "evil" behavior.

One fifth grade student stands out in my mind as my most challenging behaviorally. After twenty years and many students of different ages and grades, I still remember both his first and last name. Now, most of my students loved me and I was not considered to be a mean teacher. I tried to demonstrate my love, concern, and commitment for them every day, and I did not have favorites. Yet with this one student, about one month into the school year, and after much correction and consequences for this young man, I requested a conference with his parents. Mom came to the meeting armed with the fact that her son was very afraid of me. I had to say to his Mom that I agreed with him, and that he was wise to be afraid of me

because he consistently resisted our classroom rules and procedures, and each time that he did, I had to give him the necessary
consequences. Even though I also praised him and expressed
my love for him, since it takes eight positives for every negative,
I could not keep up with all the corrections. I did advise him in
the presence of his mom that if he did what was good, he would
have only my praise, and would never need to be afraid. She
agreed, and we continued to work with his strong character,
which I so greatly admired and desired to channel in the right
direction. The year ended, and the family moved to another
city. A few years later when I was now the principal of the
school, I was so surprised when he came to visit me and to say
thank you for helping to mold his strong character. I share this
story to emphasize the need of giving praise (rewards) to those
who do good, and to "execute wrath" (consequences) on those
who do "evil". Do not be concerned if some students fear you;
if they are doing wrong, and you are doing right, they should.

TEACH SUBMISSION FOR CONSCIENCE SAKE

Having said this, we must add that we must teach our
students to do right, not just out of fear, but as stated in verse
five of Romans thirteen, for conscience sake. It is so much more
enjoyable and peaceful to have our conscience clear, and it is
important to teach our students to do right so they can have this
peace. I remember my youngest daughter coming home one day
and telling me about the teacher needing to leave the room and
the children in order to take an injured student to the office.
She was in first grade, and teacher had a rule that if she ever left
the room, students were to continue with their work and were
not allowed to get out of their seats or talk. The little boy
behind her began to talk to her and to rock his desk back and

forth. I asked her what she did, and she said, "Mommy, I just put my head down and covered it with my arms." You see, she wanted the peace of having a clear conscience when her teacher came back into the room.

ATTENDING CONTINUALLY

A final principle regarding our positions of authority as teachers is found in Romans 13:6, where it states that people in authority are God's ministers who must attend continually to what He has called us to do. To attend continually means to be ready to correct and reward when it is convenient and when it is not; when we feel like it, and when we do not; in other words, we must be consistent in our discipline. I remember a parent conference when the student was in the room. Because I took time to prepare board work for the next day during the day, I did not allow my students to write on the chalkboard. During a conference with the parent, this student, who was very aware of our rule, proceeded to draw on the board. In front of the parent, I had to correct the student and remind him of our rule. I usually felt a little embarrassed to correct students when their parents were present, just because of their higher authority over the children than mine, but I had to attend "continually". Now this infraction was minor, but what about the situation when we are on our way to our automobile anxious to get home after a long day, and we see two students doing drugs in the parking lot, or fighting, or doing art work on the building walls? Do I "attend continually" or do I pretend not to see? In the class-room, maybe I am not feeling well today, and do not want to deal with discipline issues, do I "attend continually", or just let it go for today? Students need consistency, and if we sometimes enforce the rules and sometimes do not, they are willing to play the game of "Russian Roulette" with us. My point here is that we must be unchanging; just like God is the same yesterday, today, and forever; we must also be the same no matter what is going on in our own personal lives if we are to truly train our students to be all they can be! Consistency bears sweet fruit in our students – they know the rules and know that all must obey. They can rest in this order and feel safe and secure in the boundaries set for their good and ultimate benefit.

To conclude this section on authority, let us review its basic principles. First and foremost, discipline is a matter of authority; in order to train our students, we must understand that we are placed in positions of authority over them and therefore have the right and even the responsibility to command them. As we internalize this principle, we will manage our classes with confidence. This confidence will elicit the support of our students' parents, and will cause our students to submit to our authority over them. Again, let us remind ourselves that this authority should not be demanded or even "lorded" over our students; establishing positive relationships with our students along with teaching them the blessings of submission to authority are both crucial to the relationship that will ultimately provide that optimal learning environment. Because there is no authority unless God gives it, and those who resist authority are actually resisting the One who gives it, it is imperative that we teach our students the principles of submission to authority. As authority figures, we must not be a terror to those who are doing what is right, but only to those who do not. We must praise those who do right and give consequences to those who do not. We must teach our students to do what is right in order to have a clear and peaceful conscience. Finally, we, as teachers, must attend to our students at all times or in other words be consistent in our expectations and what we require of our students in regards to discipline.

DISCIPLINE OF STRONG WILLED, ATTENTION ON EVERYTHING, AND EXTREMELY ENERGETIC CHILDREN

Before we go into some discipline plans, I would like to take two more side notes to discuss discipline and the "strong willed" and the "hyperactive and attention deficit" child. I am not going to tell you that we need a whole new set up principles to manage children who have been blessed with wills of iron (strong willed), or those who have been blessed with the ability to focus on everything at once (attention deficit), or those who have that incredible energy that we would all like to have (hyperactive). The terms in parenthesis are those given to these students by society; they are not mine. Because of the exceptionality of these students (young or old), we must consider a few "twists" or accommodations; after all, every student has his uniqueness, and about twenty percent of the population would have these types of uniqueness.

I believe that if we understand the modalities and needs of these students, it will be easy to make a few adjustments which will make their school lives so much better and our lives likewise. First, let us consider those students who have very strong character and a natural tendency and need to have control. Some educators consider this type of student a nightmare and difficult to teach, but let us look at their qualities in a positive manner. These are the leaders, the shakers, the world changers in our midst! They are born with the strength, boldness, and courage to influence others and impact the world in which they live.

Unfortunately, it seems that our educational system would work hard to break that spirit before they become adults simply because we do not understand them and or know how to work with them. I highly recommend the work of the author, Cynthia Tobias, regarding managing this type of student. She herself was this incorrigible student, and authored a video entitled. "Who's Gonna Make Me?" I agree with her premise that there are some children who we cannot "make" do anything. So, how then do we deal with these students, be they children or adults? First, we do not go head to head with them, or one of us or probably both of us will end frustrated, angry, bloody, and wounded. Since they were born to lead and have a strong need to be in control, then we give them leadership responsibilities and even control so that we guide and even train for leadership.

How exactly do we do this? These students flourish when given responsibility, so let's give them responsibility. In the lower grades, let them be line leaders and table monitors and in charge of collecting or passing out papers. As they get older, ask them to be in charge of a certain group or assist us by helping us to know the pulse of the class or give their opinion of certain aspects of the class. I guess I understand this type of student well because I was actually one of those students, and in high school in particular I can remember being a real asset to some teachers and a real nightmare to others. I was the same person, so what made me behave one way with one teacher and contrarily with another? The answer is very simple. It was the way that some teachers managed me. When given a task or challenge, I would readily rise to the occasion, but when I felt suppressed and forced to accept a situation that could have been improved or needed changing, I remember being angry and causing problems. The success of managing me depended on how my teacher used his authority (right to manage and control).

In getting this personality type to do something, we must be willing to take the time to share the why of this activity, and an important key is to offer them choices so that they continue to feel in control. I will never forget a four year old student at lunch time. She insisted that she would eat her mango and other sweet snacks while leaving her sandwich untouched. Her desire was to finish lunch quickly so that she could go to one of the play centers set up in the room. When I figured out that putting the mango away and placing the sandwich in front of her was not going to make her eat that sandwich, I gave her a choice. You may either eat at least half of the sandwich, then the mango, and then go play; or you may eat only the sweets and remain at the table instead of playing, it is your choice. After some moments of deliberation, this very strong four year old chose to eat the sandwich, the mango, and go play. I do not think I could have "made" her eat that sandwich, but when she felt she was in control, she made the choice that both she and I could live with. In disciplining the strong willed we will need to go around (sometimes around and around and around) instead of dealing with them straight on. They must know why, and they must be given choices. I have really never met a student who when given choices says, "I will take neither." They just desire to have a say in their lives, and this is a good thing.

DISCIPLINE AND THE HYPERACTIVE OR ATTENTION DEFICIT CHILD

The subject of exceptional children will be dealt with in a later chapter, but I would like to deal with it briefly in regards to classroom discipline. I will begin this brief and very simplistic treatise of children with these challenges with a caution not to label very active students too quickly; some children are just undisciplined meaning that they have not been trained to be still or to focus on one thing. Then, there are others who, after having been instructed, trained, and coached, are unable to focus or be still. Sometimes we cannot get formal diagnosis of these challenges until students are in third or fourth grade, and by that time a lot of damage can be done because we do not understand that it is not a matter of their will, but they truly "cannot" do what we are asking of them. In these cases, it would be an injustice to give them consequences for what they do not have the ability to do. We must be careful not to wound their self-esteem by putting them in positions where they cannot succeed. Even without formal diagnosis, if we as teachers see that even after adequate instruction, training, and coaching a student is still not able to conform to what is the norm in class-rooms today, then we must make some accommodations for this student. Otherwise, he will be a constant source of frustration for us, and we will end up being a constant source of frustration for him and his parents.

The accommodations are simple; if he cannot be still, then do not require him to be. So many teachers take issue with giving these students a different treatment from all of the rest of their students, questioning whether it is fair and sometimes resenting the additional effort required of them as teachers. I want to strongly impress upon you that they are exceptional and have exceptional needs. Attempting to require the same of them as of every other student is futile and will require much more effort than making some accommodations. What kind of modifications can we make? For those who must move, allow them to move! To keep them still is like giving them poison. I remember having a first grade student who literally would spin on his head, not to get attention, but to get relief. Give these students permission to get up and walk back and forth in the back of the room; allow them to have a chair that actually rocks without the danger of tipping over; position them so that their movement will not be a distraction to others (usually front and side); make movement a part of normal instruction for every-one. Teach those "tappers" who normally drive a teacher to insanity to tap their fingers on their own thigh as a quiet way of releasing that energy. Are you getting the picture?

Now, for those students whose attention is on everything, it is important to create an environment that is as free from distractions as possible. The student described in the previous paragraph can sometimes be the worst enemy of the student who has difficulty focusing on the task at hand. Position the easily distracted student as close to you as possible so that you can bring his attention to your instruction by just touching his shoulder or mentioning his name in the same sentence as your instruction. When it is time to work independently on a task, this student may need a seat removed from the hustle and bustle of the classroom. Placing a timer on his desk to give him a reminder of the time a task must be completed is very helpful in keeping this kind of student on task. Understand that these students not only have to accomplish the task assigned, but must do so while battling their ability to focus on everything that is happening around them. I hope I have increased your awareness and given you a couple of ideas. I know that you will be able to create more solutions, and that these challenged students will breathe a sigh of relief, and that their cries of anguish, frustration, and defeat will be replaced with shouts of victory and accomplishment!

THE ROLE OF WORDS IN DISCIPLINE

I know that you are probably very anxious for me to get to the point and give you a system of discipline for your classroom, and it is my desire to give you practical ideas and skills for accomplishing discipline in the classroom. I will get to that next, but I must take one more side turn to discuss the role of our words in regards to discipline. Because we are made in the image of God, our words have the power to create, just as God's words had the power to create the earth in just six days. If we will discipline ourselves to speak what we want to see, and not what we are seeing, we will create that classroom environment that we desire. Even though others might think we are insane, when we talk about how obedient one student is, or about how peaceful and hardworking our class is, speaking the desired result will cause us and our students to believe what we are saying, and soon what we say will be what we see! I heard someone once say that before we speak, we should pause, ponder, and pray about what we will allow to come out of our mouths. Have you ever noticed that once something is said over and over, people begin to believe it? This is the case with advertising, with news reports, and with what we hear people say about any topic. If someone tells us over and over that the third grade teacher or that college professor is excellent, even though we have not personally experienced it, we believe it. This is why the Bible says that faith comes by hearing and hearing and hearing and hearing the Word of God. Faith in our students will come by both them and us hearing and hearing good things about them. Once we and they believe that they are disciplined and outstanding in every way, then they will become what they believe, and what will they believe? They will believe what we say!

Our words have the potential to re-enforce negative behaviors as we repeatedly ask the class to be quiet, to be seated or to get busy; or they can create the good behavior that we desire as we praise the one student who is doing what we ask. For example, the majority of the class is out of their seat and still talking after the tardy bell has rung. We look for those who are seated and quiet and thank them and praise them. We look up from a reading circle to thank Johnny for being busy with his seat work. The rest of the class wants to be praised, so they do the same. We do not want to begin instruction until we have everyone's attention, so we say, I will begin as soon as everyone is seated and quiet. We could say, "I am looking for the row that has their desks clear and is quiet to line up first. I am looking for someone who is sitting tall and straight with their hands folded to point to the phonics letters for the class. Our positive words create the behavior and the environment that we need.

SYSTEMS OF DISCIPLINE – INSTRUCTION, REWARDS, AND CONSEQUENCES

Now that we have laid the very important foundations of discipline and the role that understanding authority, walking in authority, and teaching authority to our students, let us move on to some practical models of discipline which we can apply in our classrooms; classrooms from pre-school through university classes. I believe that we have established the fact that teaching our students what we expect, and why it is necessary for the benefit of the whole class, is the first step. Then we can use one of many available systems to re-enforce this instruction. Most of these systems contain two major parts, rewards and consequences. I believe that a combination of both rewards for doing what is right, and consequences for not, are absolutely necessary. God, who we would agree is wiser than any human, always, always uses all three systems; instruction, rewards and consequences. First he teaches us what to do and why we should do it. He shows us what great reward we will receive or what grave consequence we will receive if we do certain things. If we are willing and obedient (instruction with desired outcome), we will eat the good of the land (reward); if we refuse and rebel, we will be cut out with the sword (consequence) (Isaiah 1:18). If we believe in Jesus Christ and confess Him with our mouths (instruction with desired outcome), we will be saved (reward); if we do not, we will be damned (consequence) (Romans 10:9).

Many systems use both rewards and consequences side by side. Both rewards and consequences are external forces, which help us to train (discipline) our students until they become self-disciplined. Our consistent instruction establishes within them the value of doing what is right, consequences and rewards help to externally train our students to do what is right, , and eventually, we reach our goal of students doing what is right, not because someone is looking over them, or for fear of consequence, or even for desire of reward. Instead, they become self-disciplined. I strongly believe that a balance of instruction, rewards and consequences is what we need to utilize, and in the following paragraphs, I will discuss some simple and effective ideas.

INSTRUCTION – KNOWLEDGE, UNDERSTANDING, AND PRACTICE OF OUR CLASSROOM BEHAVIORS

We must emphasize the importance of instruction, which includes giving our students the knowledge of what is expected, helping them to understand why certain procedures or behaviors are important, and training them over and over to behave in a certain way. The younger our students are, the more time we will need to dedicate to teaching them the behaviors we desire from them, helping them to understand why these behaviors are important for our classrooms to function, and allowing them to practice the necessary behaviors. Nevertheless, all of our students regardless of age need this instruction: knowing what we expect, why we expect it, and how they can meet our expectations. We can sometimes make the mistake of expecting behaviors before we have fully instructed our students. Of course, just as with any type of learning, this is not accomplished in one day. We will need to start right after we have begun to establish relationship with our students, and continue with this instruction until we reach the desired results in our classrooms.

For example, with elementary aged students, we have approximately five minutes between the time they enter the classroom and the time we begin pledges and announcements to accomplish many things. Therefore, we must make our expectations and the reasons for them very clear to our students. We will also have to practice a number of times before our class will be able to take care of all of this business in just five minutes. We begin by explaining that we have only five minutes to take care of getting ready for the day, ordering lunch, and taking attendance as the announcements and pledges will begin at exactly 8:05am. It is important for us to be ready so that we can give our full attention to the announcements, explaining why they are very important for us. We might put a list of things to do on the board as follows (for non-reading children pictures work very well):

1. Come in quietly, sit down, unpack your bag, and take out assignment book or folder, copy homework.

2. When your row is called put your lunch, book bag, and coat away and line up at teacher's desk with your assignment folder. If you are buying lunch, write your name on lunch order and hand to teacher when she checks your folder.

3. Sharpen your pencils (2); pick up paper and seat work; return to your desk to finish copying assignments and begin seatwork.

4. Be quiet, be busy, and stay in your seat until your row is called.

The first week of class, we might have to walk our students through this procedure every day; the key is to do it until they are fully trained in it. We might add some rewards for the row that does the best job or the individual who is ready the quickest. After about a week, we might add some consequences for not being quite ready on time.

You may be protesting at this point and asking what this has to do with classroom management. Classroom management and discipline encompass everything that is necessary to have a well-functioning class; it is not just having a quiet class. It is all of those things which allow us to expediently and effectively teach our students. When we can complete our pre-instruction activities in five minutes, and our students are prepared for instruction, we have more time, and an environment of order in which to teach.

Is this type of management also necessary for high school or even college students? You probably already know that I am going to say, yes. Once the tardy bell rings, and while we are taking attendance, our expectations might be the following:

1. All students are seated and no longer talking without permission

2. Today's homework is on the desk

3. Tomorrow's homework is copied

4. Students are reviewing yesterday's notes.

Again, even with older students, we will need to instruct the students on what we desire and why we desire it. Then we will also have to practice the procedure or behaviors desired until they master them. We can also add both incentives and consequences to motivate our students externally until the desired behaviors become internally motivated. Instruction, which includes explaining the "what's" and "why's" and running our students through a few practice sessions is a vital key to great discipline and classroom management. We can only expect what we have taught, and rewards and consequences will help our students establish internal habits of behaviors that will benefit the entire class and ultimately their work group or community or country.

REWARDS

Now, let's discuss the most pleasant tool for establishing great classroom behaviors, rewards. It is part of our nature to desire to be praised and rewarded. Though we should not have to be paid to do what is right, rewards are handy tools that will help us train our students in the habit of doing right. Rewards do not cost anything, so use them abundantly! They come in many forms and are effective motivators for students from ages one to eighty. They need not be costly, and can range from a public praise, to a private thank you, to less homework, to an encouraging note, to extra time at recess, to a sticker, to getting to help teacher, to wearing the sheriff badge to a positive phone call to Dad or Mom. There is no limit to the rewards we can create, the key is to understand that rewards re-enforce behaviors until those behaviors become habits, which lead to self-discipline. Obviously, as students mature, they become more and more self-disciplined, lessening the need for systems of rewards, but never the need for the reward of praise and acknowledgement.

We want to be very generous with this exciting tool of rewarding our students because rewards are so effective, and they cost us nothing but a little effort. Take pleasure in blessing your students bountifully with rewards. Seek every opportunity to reward especially those who need the most training and discipline. This may mean really "digging for gold" with the most challenging students, and when you find it, it will be such a reward to you as their teacher to see the great transformation in them because you searched for and found value in them.

TANGIBLE OR VISIBLE REWARD SYSTEMS

In addition to verbal rewards, tangible or visible representations of rewards such as points on the board, or marbles in jars, or paper strips, or even pennies are very effective with students of all ages. I will explain a couple, and you can use your own imagination to create or even change your system every quarter or every month. Let's use the point or penny system. This can either be done by rows or tables, and encourages teamwork and puts some training responsibility on team members; or it may be done individually. Team names or row numbers are put on the chalk board; a glass jar could be prepared for each team (Pennies make a lot of noise when dropped in the jar; this noise gets the attention of the others who will mimic the behavior to earn their penny). If you desire to work on individuals and not teams, then individual names would need to be put on a poster board as they would take up too much room on the chalkboard. The desired behavior would be rewarded and thus re-enforced by giving a mark to the appropriate team, or by dropping a penny in a teams' jar. Use verbal recognition along with the written or tangible points, and the other teams or individuals will again imitate the desired behavior. At the end of the day, or week, or semester (the younger the students, the more immediate the reward should be), tally the points or count the pennies, and give that row the reward (they get to be first to line up all the next day, or they get five less homework problems, or they get two extra points on the final, etc...) Using coins will re-enforce the use of money, using roman numerals would re-enforce their use; in other words, we can take advantage of our discipline incentives to re-enforce academic subjects. For younger students, placing a smiling face on their desk while verbally praising the desired behavior will get all the students working for the same reward. The key is to reward the positive behavior rather than verbally admonish the negative behavior, as positive rewards are much more effective than negative consequences.

CONSEQUENCES

I do believe that consequences are also a vital component of any discipline system, as they teach our students a very valuable life lesson; actions good or bad bring consequences. If their actions are good, then the rewards will be good, and if their actions are negative, then the reward will also be negative. Making sure that there are negative consequences for negative behavior is an external means of training our students to do what is right. It is also a Biblical principle. Though God does not punish us for wrong doing, when we do wrong, negative consequences result. If I do not desire to get a speeding ticket, then I must drive the speed limit; if I do not desire to be reprimanded by the teacher, then I must obey the teacher's rules.

We can even use our reward systems to issue consequences. For example, one member of a team is misbehaving; we take one point away from the team. This will usually cause other team members to admonish or encourage the team member to do what is right. We could teach true team work by giving the entire team five additional points for their positive encouragement of the team member, or we could explain the effectiveness of positive encouraging words and reluctantly take some additional points off. Using the smiling face example, we could also have a frowning face to let the student know that we are not pleased with the behavior. With consequences, I would rarely publicly verbally issue the consequence, unless the entire group would benefit from the admonishment. Our desire is to encourage our students and edify them. Correction in front of the entire class does not usually accomplish this goal. It is more effective to ask them to step outside the classroom, or talk with you after class, or to just whisper the admonishment in the student's ear. I would suggest that public corrections be used only when the entire group would benefit from the admonishment as in the case of a student publicly challenging the authority of a person in authority. Even in this case, the student should be corrected in love and with respect.

LOVE AND LOGIC IN DISCIPLINE

Another key element to consequences is making the student responsible for his/her actions. There is a complete course regarding this type of discipline and I highly recommend the book by Jim Fay and David Funk entitled *Teaching with Love and Logic.* There are two basic principles in this plan of teaching with love and logic; love and logic. In order to discipline with love, we must show empathy for our students and the situation they have put themselves into due to wrong choices. We are very sorry that they have chosen to disrespect their fellow student, but we strive to remain calm, happy, and free from anger ourselves. This is disciplining with love both for us and for our students. We have to demonstrate our love for ourselves by not getting angry and frustrated, and for our students by telling them how sorry we are that they have put themselves in this situation. The second part of this very effective discipline plan is to use logic. Both we and our students will have to think and reason regarding the consequences of their choices. As our students make good or bad choices, we allow them to reap either the rewards or the consequences.

If they make a wise choice, there should be a reward; if not, there should be a consequence. The consequences should be for them and not for us as their teachers. If I keep a high school student after school, then I suffer the consequence of having to stay late, but if I have him sit in the classroom during lunch instead of socializing with his friends, then only he endures the consequence. Consequences help teach our students to be responsible for their actions and their choices. I once had a high school student throw a gang sign when the class group picture was taken. The photographer noticed and did not make the prints, but various students had paid for the picture and wanted one. I called the student in and explained "her" problem to her and asked her what she was going to do about it. She had no idea, but was very apologetic insisting that she was not a gang member. I asked her if she wanted some suggestions and she said yes. She thought she might be expelled, but that would not solve the problem of the class's picture being ruined. I suggested that the picture could be retaken, but that would involve a lot of work and even some money to pay the photographer for returning to the school. The young lady agreed that she would call the photographer to request the retake; pay for the re-shoot time and mileage; unload, set-up, and load all of the equipment; write the letter to the parents regarding the reason for and time of the re-take; and encourage all of the students to arrive before school so that additional class time was not wasted. This consequence was much more severe than a one or two day suspension, and taught the student much more. I am a very firm believer of the power of holding students responsible for their choices, and insuring that they receive the teaching that consequences provide. In summary, this consequence took a lot of logical thinking to create, and taught this student to think carefully before acting – the logic part of "Love and Logic" teaching.

If I am training my students to be disciplined about completing their homework, then I cannot allow them to turn it in the next day without a substantial grade deduction (consequence). If I am training my second graders to remember their coats when leaving for lunch and recess, and one leaves theirs in the classroom, I cannot allow them to return to the classroom for it; they will learn more from being outside for fifteen minutes without it. This may seem like a no "love" consequence, but it works as it forces students to use their logic (reasoning brought about by consequences) to figure out how not to get into this situation again! You might ask, "Where is the love?" The love is expressed through our empathy about the situation the student is in, and in the fact that we love them so much we require for them to take responsibility for their choices. It makes students victors over situations and not victims of circumstances.

We want to balance the love and logic in this form of discipline. When dealing with discipline issues, never allow the behavior of a student to upset you. If you do, then who is experiencing the consequence, you or them? Be empathetic with the student who has broken the rule or not met the assignment and express freely that empathy. Do not take responsibility for their choice or action. Instead, express your empathy for their situation, and then ask them what they are going to do about the problem; this requires them to think logically. Make some suggestions if they would like some, or have them continue to think about solutions until they figure one out that is acceptable to both you and them. Then, make sure they fulfill the consequences.

Here is another simple example; a student forgets their research paper at home, and it is due today. Should we allow them to call their parents at work or home and punish them by having them drop everything and "helicopter in" the paper? Remember that our goal is for our students to experience the consequence. We could sincerely express our sorrow that they forgot it; even acknowledging that we ourselves have forgotten things in the past, and ask them what they should do. We ask them to figure out a solution in which there is a consequence. We do not take the responsibility from them. They could make sure that the paper gets to us by a certain time that day, or by the next day with a deduction, or add another section with a lesser deduction. Let them propose a solution that is acceptable to both of you. In this way, they will learn from the experience; otherwise, either we or their parents are inconvenienced by their situation and receive the consequence, and they will learn nothing.

When using this love and logic method of training, we must not lose our tempers or raise our voices. Doing so puts the consequence on us and takes it off of our students. If we deal with discipline issues very systematically and very constantly, we will never (almost) lose it. After all, it is their problem and not ours. When we feel that we are reaching "boiling point", let's give that student or the entire class a time out to allow us and our students to think logically about the situation, then we can return to the situation and deal with it both with love and with logic. At first, our students will be frustrated at having to deal with their own problems, but it is amazing how well this love and logic technique works. Our students learn to be responsible for their actions and we will continue to enjoy our vocation as teachers.

DETERRING DISCIPLINE PROBLEMS THROUGH PREPARATION, ORGANIZATION, AND DYNAMIC TEACHING

There are three other factors which will greatly deter discipline problems. The first, and one of the best, is for us to be prepared academically and spiritually. Utilizing what we learned about preparation in chapter three, we know where we are going and how we will get there. Our objectives are clear, and we have written plans on how we will achieve them. We have also studied our material so that we can present it in a clear, interesting and exciting way. In addition, we have taken the time to pray for guidance and discernment and wisdom for ourselves and for the peace, obedience and understanding of our students. Really, there is nothing that creates more discipline problems than when we are not as prepared as we ought to be. Our students can always tell, and never fail to take advantage of us when our lack of preparation is exposed. Therefore, let's be prepared, and thus avoid discipline issues.

Organizing and managing our class time is another way to avoid discipline problems. When we have our class period broken down into time segments; we can move from one segment and activity to the next with very little "down time" in between transitions. Most discipline issues seem to occur during transition times or "down time"; not when we are teaching, but when we are moving from one activity to another; putting away our language books and preparing to begin history, or preparing to take the exam, or dismissing for the day. With this in mind, we need to avoid a lot of "down time", and take full advantage of the time that we have both to teach and to allow our students to interact with the material taught. Substitutes will always appreciate a full lesson with much to accomplish rather than trying to keep a class in control during "study hall". In addition, we must make our expectations very clear when moving into a transition time. For a university class, "We will be taking a fifteen minute break; you may leave the classroom; there are snack machines down the hall; be here at 9:15." For a high school class, "Now that we have completed the review, please clear your desk of everything except a cover sheet and a pen; once you receive your exam, there will be no more talking to anyone except me and that with permission." For an elementary class, "Without talking, please pass your papers to the person in front of you using your right hand; the first person please take your paper to the last person; take out a pen; be ready by the time I say one, five, four, three, two, one; I will read the correct answer;

if it is wrong put an "x" on the number, if correct do nothing." Can you see how keeping "down time" to a minimum and giving clear instructions of our expectations during transitions will alleviate discipline problems?

The third effective factor that deters discipline problems is excellent teaching. What exactly is excellent teaching? That is the topic of the next chapter. I am so excited about the next chapter entitled "Teach, Teach, Teach – Six Steps to Success." As we learn the techniques of excellent teaching, our students will be so captivated by what and how we teach, that they will have no desire to act in a negative way!

We have laid an excellent foundation of principles of good discipline. I hope that knowing, understanding, and applying the principles of being both under and in authority; the principles of instruction, training, and coaching; the principles of rewards, and consequences; the principles of love and logic; along with the other key points of this chapter will be of much value to us as we create with them the atmosphere of respect and order which will help our students to learn. As I have mentioned, if we cannot control our students, then we cannot teach them. We must invest time especially at the beginning of our year or semester to teach and train these principles, but this investment will eventually save us a lot of time and a lot of frustration. We will add these principles of discipline to the principles studied in the previous chapters – Our vocation, the what and why of teaching; Touching to teach, the role of establishing positive relationships with our students; Preparing to teach, the act of mapping our destination or goals for the year, semester, quarter and day. Now let us get on our way to the very exciting topic of teaching methods; another vital ingredient to the training of individuals who are the future of our nations who will become positive change instruments of our society.

APPLICATION (WISDOM)

1. *Share the authority principle with a co-worker and keep each other accountable to be both under and in authority.*

2. *Teach the authority principle to your students*

3. *Determine the most challenging moments regarding discipline and invest the time establishing and teaching the behaviors and procedures which will alleviate that disorderly time in your schedule.*

4. *Practice showing empathy and requiring your students to determine and fulfill consequences that will help them be "non-repeaters" of offenses.*

5. *Inventory the last week you taught and the most challenging classroom management times; note whether the problems were due to lack of organization, dynamic teaching, preparation, or training.*

Chapter Five

SIX STEPS TO SUCCESS

Key Points

1. *Inspire our students to get them ready to learn by praying for them, having them say positive things about themselves, sharing a wise saying, or giving them a brain teaser.*

2. *Review in a dynamic, fast paced and interesting way to re-establish what was taught yesterday and the day before and the day before and the day before.*

3. *Instruct by telling, showing and letting our students; keeping it simple; and guiding them in practicing what we have taught them.*

4. *Allow students to begin their independent practice in class and finish it at home to insure that they are applying what they have learned.*

5. *Review one more time at the end of class to make sure that those "bricks" are laid straight.*

6. *Bless the students and give them those "last words" that will stick with them until you see them again.*

Now that we have laid a very solid foundation of why we teach (we are called to transform lives), of the need to relate to students and touch their hearts to teach them, of the criticalness of preparing to teach, and of the need for discipline to teach, I am so excited about getting into some chapters on teaching methodology that will cause your students to learn and not forget what they learn! What a great goal – to teach so that all of our students actually learn, understand, and are able to apply what is taught! These are truly viable and reachable goals. In this chapter we will discuss six easy steps that will help you to accomplish them. There really are some components or steps that, when added to the principles that we learned in the previous chapters, will honestly cause all of your students to learn and not forget what they learned!

This chapter is one that is very exciting for me as you can see from all of the exclamation points in the previous paragraph. With my passion and my love of teaching, whether my students are my own children, three year olds at church, high school students, adult students of English or Spanish as a second language, or even teachers, I believe that I have been an effective teacher. My measuring stick of that effectiveness is whether or not my students were able to actually apply to real life situations the knowledge I was attempting to give them. Although evaluation in the form of written exams, oral presentations, and projects are necessary measures, the bottom line for me has always been what my students are able to do with the knowledge I have attempted to give them. I have had to ask if those first graders, after I taught them their many phonics rules, could actually decode letters to read. Could those Spanish students actually carry on a conversation in Spanish and communicate in writing? Could those teachers actually attain the environment in a classroom through class management to actually be free to teach? I have found the answer to be yes for any student who would actually physically show up for class. If they were in class physically, I could get them in class mentally, emotionally, and even spiritually. How is this possible? You may even be a little skeptical, even thinking, "Who does she think she is how can this be?"

I do not take credit for what I am going to share with you in this chapter. These six steps or vital components of teaching were revealed to me when I first began to teach. Without knowing it at the time, they are what made my teaching successful. Actually I feel that I have taught all of my life; I was always a teacher, even when I was a child I was teaching others, and when I began to teach teachers, the very first workshop outline I presented was on these six steps. Since that time, I have taught this workshop over and over and even in different countries, and I continue to receive the feedback that this seminar has consistently and dramatically changed the results that teachers get in their classrooms. Incredibly, I was never taught these steps in a university methods class, yet I have realized that they were what have made my teaching effective over the years. They are very simple, and I will share them with you in plain English so that they are easy to remember. I guarantee that if you use them every day in every class that you teach, your students will truly learn and be able to apply what you teach. Many of you are probably already using these steps and are not aware of it, but the key will be that you must use them every day and in every class if you want to be an effective teacher, one whose students learn and are able to apply what is taught.

Let's begin with a riddle that my own children asked me years ago. It was probably my oldest daughter who is very wise and witty who asked me, "Mom, how do you eat an elephant?" To this I answered that I would not like to eat an elephant because

I would expect that elephant meat would be very tough if we measure it by the looks of their outer skin. Of course she insisted that I must give her an answer, and when I could not give her the right one, she took great joy in telling me that you eat an elephant one bite at a time; funny, but true. As with anything that we eat, we must eat it one bite at a time. We cannot stuff the entire steak, or cookie or candy, or even elephant in our mouths at once, or soon it will be coming right back out. Yet, we as educators sometimes try to feed our students the entire elephant in one major, huge serving! This will just not work.

I wish we could be face to face in a seminar right now. I would demonstrate this point. I love to bring elephants made of about four large marshmallows to my workshop. One person must eat the entire elephant in one bite; another is allowed to eat the elephant piece by piece. Need I ask which of my student teachers enjoyed their elephant more, or which was able to keep the elephant in their stomachs or which one had to spit it up in the trash can? Believe me, the only way to eat an elephant is one bite at a time, and the only way to teach students is one bite at a time; line upon line and precept or principle upon principle! Now, let's see how we break up our subject matter and present it to our students, one "bite" at a time, laying one principle upon the previous one, which has been made solid by the techniques or six steps which we will discuss next.

STEP NUMBER ONE: INSPIRATION, BECAUSE OUR STUDENTS CANNOT LEARN UNTIL THEY ARE AT EASE

According to brain research, and as I mentioned in a previous chapter, our brains will not allow us to receive knowledge, understanding, and wisdom until we are totally comfortable with the source. It is as though we have an internal mechanism built in to prevent entrance until the source has been validated; kind of like the firewalls of our computers. Therefore, it is very important for us to begin each class by opening up this "firewall" and getting the brain's approval to transmit the information. In addition to working consistently on a relationship of love, trust, and commitment with our students, daily, before we begin to teach, we must re-inspire our students. This step is done within two to three minutes, and will set the excellent environment which we need to truly teach our students. How can we inspire them; ignite their desire to learn; encourage them; interest them? We will want to start each day or class with something that is positive and uplifting such as prayer, positive words, a serious brain teaser, or even some salt to make our students thirsty.

Let's look at each of these ideas more carefully. Let's begin class with prayer. Let's acknowledge God and ask for His wisdom and the guidance of the Holy Spirit. Let's pray for excellent, interesting, dynamic, witty teaching and for students who are alert and bright and intelligent. Let's pray against distractions and for our students' sound minds and ability to do all things. Let's give God the things that concern us, knowing that He perfects them. Do you get the picture? I do caution here that praying can become rote and a vain repetition unless you and your students work to "really pray" with faith and not just say words. For those of you who are not legally allowed to pray formally, you can still do so informally. Just say something like this, "We are going to have a great day filled with the most dynamic and interesting teaching. I believe that each student will benefit by today's lesson and that we have a great time learning today. Let's choose to put those worries out of our minds for now." Then you can silently add, "In Jesus name, Amen."

Another very powerful inspirational tool is to have students actually stand while saying some very positive statements about the class such as, "Today we will have the best class of the year. Our teacher has a strong teaching gift and is able to place line upon line until we totally learn the material. We are intelligent and retain everything that we learn. We can do this work, and we will enjoy doing it!" (Sample #5)

To inspire our students, we can also give them a "brain teaser" while we take attendance; we put a question on the board which will get those brain juices flowing. Movement and song can also inspire. Sharing a devotional (short inspirational story or wise saying for those who are not allowed to use the Bible) will also inspire and motivate our students to learn. We could also inspire by going to the front of the room and just telling our class how much we believe in them and praise them for their hard work and attentiveness. I know that you will be able to add some of your own creative ideas to these. The principle is that we do not start teaching until our students are ready to learn. How can a student learn when he or she is worried about Mom and Dad who just had an argument in the car over finances, or when our adult students are concerned about their own children? Inspire first, and get ready for the most exciting, interesting, effective classes you have ever taught!

And now we are ready to teach? Not! Before we can teach our new material, we must go to step number two, which is review.

STEP NUMBER TWO: REVIEW, BECAUSE NOTHING IS LEARNED IN ONE DAY

Step or component number two is to review. We must understand that nothing, nothing, nothing is learned (as we have defined learning; knowledge, understanding, and wisdom or application) in one day, or in one sitting, or after having presented it one time. Many times, teachers do a wonderful job of preparing their lesson and teaching it. Then the next day and lesson, they again do a great job of presenting another topic in an interesting and simplified way, and so on and so on for each lesson for the entire year, yet their students are not able to apply what is taught. Why is this? Because lesson after lesson is placed upon the previous lesson without insuring that the students learned what was actually taught, and that the previous concept was actually cemented before adding the next layer of instruction. Let's compare this to laying a brick wall, and each day's lesson represents another layer of bricks. Well, if by chance one of the bricks from the previous day ended up being circular instead of rectangular, or our students understood half of what we taught so the brick was triangular, or they just did not get the subject presented, there will be a missing brick; then when we lay the next layer of bricks, they will certainly topple and fall. This is why it is vitally important to review daily before trying to teach new material.

I hope that you are now convinced that we must review in order to solidify the concepts which we previously taught. So the next question is, "What do we review?" Well we review what we taught the previous day and the day before that day, and the day before that and the day before that and the day before that... This review should include the material taught from the first day of a unit or chapter to the material taught the last day of the unit. Review should even include concepts taught in previous units. Why? Again I say this because no one learns anything in one day. We have to be sure that our students actually learned the previous days' (days', not day's) material.

How many days or even years did it take each one of us to communicate verbally? How many times did our parents review the proper way of sitting or eating? How many times did we have to cook something before we were able to make that delicious lasagna or roast or casserole? Yet so often in school, we do expect our students to be able to do long division, or balance chemical equations, or use proper grammar, or know the events of world wars after having presented the material once or twice. Good curriculums actually build in this review, and purposefully spiral the learning of concepts by setting introduction, review and mastery goals in three year intervals. Because we as teachers want our students to really learn (have the ability to apply concepts) we must build review into our daily lessons. One might say, "If I do this, then I will never finish the curriculum which I must cover by the end of the year." On the contrary, not only will we finish the curriculum, our students will have learned it and learned it for life. Wouldn't that be a revolutionary concept? How is this possible? Consistent and thorough review will accomplish our goal of learning not just for the exam, but long term, and will also avoid the painful and costly time of remediation later.

The next question is, "When do we review?" Again, let me emphasize that we must review daily. Have you ever taught a well prepared lesson only to find that when you finish, five to ten hands or even the entire class stared at you with that look of confusion? Have you ever taught then realized that the light bulbs did not all turn on? Or have you ever taught a concept, then given an assignment only to find that over half of the students could not do the assignment independently, and you had to go to student after student to go over the concept again.

How much time does it take to then go back and teach each of those students independently? Have you ever taught an idea over a period of time and come to evaluation time only to find that over half of the students had not mastered the concept, and worse yet that over half received a grade of 69% and below? These scores reflected that even though students received a passing grade (usually 61% or more); they are still lacking mastery of as much as 39% of the material. When this happens, we generally just continue to teach new material. Unfortunately, the solid wall of bricks which we are trying to lay is faulty, and due to the lack of the solid foundations, students struggle with the next concept, and sometimes struggle with the subject (math for example), for the rest of their school years.

So, to answer the question of when to review – we must review daily. Before we teach that new concept, let's be sure that the previous layer of bricks is nice and even. In addition to reviewing before we teach a new concept, we should also stop and review while teaching new concepts. If you use outline formatting for your notes, this would mean to review minimally after each Roman numeral. If you use power point presentations, review at the end of each slide, etc... Review during instruction insures that you keep those bricks in an even line before you add too many more. Finally, review at the end of daily instruction to enable students to apply the concepts independently after you have taught.

So to summarize, we review before instructing new material to help our students thoroughly grasp yesterday's material. We review at various times during the instruction of new material to help our students to re-affirm smaller blocks of material. And finally, we review at the end of our day's instruction to further assist our students in applying what they have learned.

At this point, you may be thinking, "Review, review, review. If I do all of this review, how will I ever have the time to reach all of my learning objectives? Basically, you are asking, "How do I review?" Review means to look again at a concept that has already been taught in detail; it is important to note that review does not mean re-teach. If we re-teach, we will certainly not have time to teach new material, and we will probably bore our students. During review, our students do all of the talking and we do the asking or guiding. We review by very briefly asking our students to verbalize or demonstrate what we have taught. We do not re-teach. Pre-instructional review should take a maximum of five to seven minutes. During instruction review should take about a minute, and after instruction review, a maximum of two minutes. Review must be dynamic, meaning that different formats must be used each time. One day review could be asking questions about yesterday's material; another day review could be a five minute group contest to see which group could list the most facts learned; or it could consist of actually doing a mathematical problem writing out in words each step; a different review could be having the class explain a process or concept with every student verbally adding one part or step. Enhance this exciting, yet valuable review time by adding a little competition with some sort of incentive for the individual or group with the best or most answers, and we have students learning things that they will never forget! Reciting or memorizing information to a musical tune or to a rhythm will also put information in memory that will stay with a student forever. The key to good review is that it be dynamic, interesting, fast paced, challenging, and even fun.

Rote memorization versus higher level thinking argument

Before proceeding to the "how to's" of review or drill, let us dissolve an argument that some of you may have already considered; the argument that review or drill and memorization is useful only for the purpose of regurgitating facts and figures, but does not involve higher level thinking skills, and seems too rote. This is a widely held argument amongst educators that I would like to dispel by returning to the concept of knowledge, understanding, and wisdom. Review helps our students to acquire knowledge; the repetitiveness of it causes understanding; as I mentioned earlier, nothing is learned in one day, light bulbs or "ah ha's" happen at different times for different people. Wisdom is the application of the knowledge and understanding that our students gain; the ability to take information and do something with it.

I must stress here that without knowledge and understanding regarding a subject, our students cannot exercise their higher level thinking skills. In history, for example, students must know the events that led up to a particular war along with its time line of events before having the ability to analyze that war and come to the deductions of how that war might have been prevented or even compare that war with a current one. In mathematics, students must have learned thoroughly those addition and multiplication tables before gaining the ability to solve word problems with the use of one or two variable equations. Before being able to put together a "Power Point " presentation, I will first need to know the basics of adding a slide or adding sound or color to a slide. Our goal is always going to be application of understood knowledge, but review is a key to the acquisition of such. With this argument disputed, let us return to the basic skills of review.

Review must involve everyone and should move from large groups to smaller groups to individuals

It is important to note here that review must involve everyone and especially those students who need additional time to fully understand or remember concepts and ideas. Therefore, we must design our review in such a way that we insure that the students, who need the most review, get the most practice with the material. When reviewing, or "drilling", you are almost like the conductor of an orchestra moving from everyone playing to allowing a section of drummers to have a solo, back to the entire orchestra, then to a flute solo, etc...

When reviewing a concept that is not so familiar, have everyone answer in unison; repeat the answer so that those who did not know could hear the correct response. Then move to smaller groups, again so that those a little more challenged can hear it again. Finally, move to individuals. When we are at the individual level, which individual do you suspect we should call upon, those waving their hands, or those hiding out so that we do not call upon them? Right, those who are not raising their hands are the ones who need more review, so let's call on them most often. You might object, but if they do not know, we will embarrass them, and even waste much time waiting for them to respond. We would be surprised at how much these students do know; it is usually their lack of confidence or interest that impedes them from raising their hands. Nevertheless, to avoid a possible painful situation, and to engage every student, anytime you call on someone and they are unable to answer within five to seven seconds (comfortable thinking and waiting time), just ask the group or another individual (the one flailing his hands in the air) to help out. Once they have given the correct answer, then return to the individual and have him repeat it now that he has heard the correct answer.

Start with the familiar and move to the unfamiliar

When reviewing, always warm that wonderful brain up by starting with the most recent and most familiar material. This boosts confidence and gets review off to a quick and therefore interesting pace. It is also acceptable when a concept is first being reviewed to allow students to refer to their notes or yours. They would not be able to review effectively without them because the material has not yet been mastered. The key is to give them many opportunities to interact with material in order for them to retain and gain understanding of the information and concepts. Of course, eventually the concepts should be reviewed with our students utilizing strictly what is in their memory. We discussed earlier that we should review daily the material that we have taught in the entire unit or chapter, and even that from a previous one (I am a strong supporter of quarter, mid-term, and semester exams as they require students to retain concepts in a course and not learn just for a chapter test). Most of our five to seven minute review time should be spent on the material which is not yet familiar to our students or that material which we taught in the previous class. From here, we move backwards in our notes to the day before, then the day before, and the day before reviewing very briefly those concepts taught at the beginning of a unit as they are going to be well mastered if we have followed this review plan consistently. Because we have reviewed for a few minutes daily, we will not need to spend days reviewing for an evaluation, or hours working on review sheets.

The skill of review questions and the time spent on reviewing a taught concept

Effective review is fast paced, interesting, student active, and all students encompassing. Another important skill for us to learn is the art of review questions, and the amount of review time spent on a concept in a five day period. During a review of not yet mastered material, allow students to interact with the material at least three times, and in three different ways. Example: yesterday, we taught the digestive system and the path that food takes from the mouth to elimination. I want my students to interact with this material at least three times during the review, so I start by asking a student (those that like to be center of attention) to come to the front and point to and help the students to follow the path of that hamburger they had for lunch (mouth, esophagus, stomach, small intestine, large intestine, anus). Then I might ask table one to tell what happens to food in each of those areas as another group lists them one by one. Finally, I might have each row, as a group; list the chemical reactions that occur in each section. On our first day of review for this concept, we have allowed our students to interact with the material three times. I review the same material three times, but in three different ways. Since I just taught this material yesterday, we will allow students to use their notes during today's review, but since we reviewed thoroughly today, tomorrow we will ask the same types of questions without the use of notes, and with much less detail. The third day we review this material, we might just have them work in teams and give them one minute to write on the board as many things as they know about the digestive system with points to the team with the most complete list. On the fourth day, while we check attendance, we might just add some critical thinking to their review of this material by asking each student to write an explanation of why someone got sick after having popcorn, coke, nachos and a hot dog at the theatre. Since on day two to five we will probably cover other concepts that will need to be reviewed, we will devote less of our review time to this concept each day, but want to daily ask a couple of questions about it. A hint to remembering what needs to be reviewed is to have our notes in outline format and easily accessible during review. Having the vital few concepts in outline format on cards or even on power point make reviewing interesting, fast paced and effective. It is very difficult to review using a text, because there is just too much information on too many pages to be able to pull out those vital few concepts readily.

Variation, fast pace, competition, and rhythm make review interesting and effective

Can anyone teach a sleeping giant, or a sleeping anything for that matter? Probably not; therefore, we must engage our students, or they will not learn, understand, retain and eventually apply the material we teach them (knowledge, understanding and wisdom). Our review must be varied, fast paced, competitive, and even rhythmic in order to make it interesting and effective. Changing it up daily in order to keep the interest of our students may take some effort when we first begin to review effectively, but once we practice some of these techniques, we will be able to spontaneously choose a mode for daily review. The key is to use a variety of techniques and to remember that during review, our role is facilitative. Here is a list of review ideas that will work with students of all ages, and with any subject you are teaching:

1. Simply ask questions and have students give answers from a chart or notes.

2. Have students repeat what you say adding a snap, pop, or jump. ("12 (snap) times 12 (snap); 24 (clap, or bend knees, or jump), 24 (clap, jump, or bend knees).

3. Sing the steps of digestion from the ingestion to excretion to the tune of a familiar song, or better yet have them create a rap.

4. Play charades having students give clues for the title and author of the literary pieces studied thus far in English.

5. Put geometry, algebra, trig problem on the board and have students work in teams to solve; first finished with correct answer does five less homework problems; all finished and correct do two less homework problems.

6. Give students five minutes to research a topic and site the references found in APA format.

7. Tell the story of the American Revolution as taught so far with each student adding one fact to the story

8. Girls against boys spelling bee type competition; first to answer correctly remains standing, other is eliminated and must record all given answers and questions.

9. Demonstrate the use of rewards and consequences in discipline by dividing into groups and assigning one individual as the teacher and others the students.

10. In five minutes, show your class mates how to do long division, or diagram gerunds and infinitives, or call 911 for help.

Next, we must keep our review time at a very fast pace. This will help students to require the quick retrieval of information from their long and short term memories. It will also stimulate them so that they remain alert during review time. To help keep the pace up, ask questions rapidly and require the students to reply rapidly. Slow questions and slowly spoken answers will cause boredom and allow students to disengage.

Rhythm in questioning and in responding will also keep the pace up. Remember not to wait more than five to seven seconds for a response from an individual as long pauses also allow students to disengage. During review, all students must be responding verbally or in any other format at least every five to seven seconds. Therefore both our questions and our students' answers must come within this time frame. Keeping a fast pace will also enable us to cover the maximum amount of material within our five to seven minute pre-instruction, one minute during instruction, and two minute after instruction review times.

Competition also aids in keeping our students engaged. I will share some of my favorites for each learner area, and then let your imaginations be the guide for more. Younger students love contests between individuals or rows. A favorite is "popcorn" with girls against boys. The teacher asks a question, and the first boy or girl to pop up and then give the answer once acknowledged wins a point for the team. Since competitive games are so much fun that we do not want to stop, we could set a timer for the five to seven minutes allotted to review time. In order to give everyone a chance to respond, once a kernel has popped, it has to wait for all the others to pop before getting to pop again. To keep the already popped kernels engaged, they could continue writing the correct answers, and win an individual prize for the person with the most correct answers. The winning team could win an extra five minutes at recess, or accumulate points and receive a one day homework pass.

Older students love to participate in competitions, which involve some sort of athletic skill. We can play "nerf" basketball requiring a student to respond correctly for a chance to shoot a basket. Again to keep all involved, those not up to shoot, write the answers and when they have five to ten, they can stand at the free throw line and shoot. The team with the most games won in a week could win an added three points on the next exam. Note that the incentives are costless, and that the younger the students are, the more immediate the rewards need to be.

There is a favorite competition of all ages called "Around the world"; it involves individuals competing to answer the question the fastest. The winner proceeds to the next individual; at the end of our review time limit, the student who has proceeded to the most number of seats is the winner. We can use our wonderful imaginations to think of a desirable incentive for the "King of the world". Again, in order to have everyone engaged those who are not responding verbally could write the answer in a complete sentence and when they have ten correct answers could challenge the current contestant. You might be thinking that those are cute games for elementary and high school students, but what about adult learners. I do not believe that we ever outgrow the desire to compete and to have fun, and we can do this while learning! How about a game of trivia, hangman, charades, or wheel of fortune where correct explanations of concepts allow us to guess a letter to the puzzle which is part of what we are studying? Again, we can use our incredible imaginations to design competitive ways to review material we have taught our students, and thus help them to retain valuable information.

The last way to make our review interesting and dynamic is to use rhythm during review. Use clapping and snapping and hip shaking to review information. Add a little hop between syllables when reviewing spelling words; add two claps to the end of each answer; sway to the left and the right as punctuation rules are reviewed. Sing information to a well-known tune, or to a currently popular song. It is amazing how rhythm and movement help difficult information get in and stay in our wonderful brains, and how recalling the song or rhythm helps our brains to find that information quickly!

An entire book could be written about the review process, but I believe that you are learning some principles and techniques which will be very useful to help your students learn, understand, and apply valuable information. And now, we can finally teach!

STEP NUMBER THREE: INSTRUCTION, PRESENTATION, OR TEACHING

Now that our students have been inspired or motivated and now that we are sure that those foundations that we laid yesterday and the day before and the day before are solid, we are finally ready to teach. Steps one and two took a maximum of ten very well spent minutes. Do you remember the chapter three principles regarding preparing to teach? We have done our homework by studying and outlining and breaking down our subject matter into simple and logical segments. We have our lesson plan and know the objectives for this day, and now, on to what we were born to do! I get excited just thinking about this step!

Let's start by laying a very important principle to follow when teaching anything. Students have different learning styles and strengths; some depend more on their visual strengths, others on what they hear, others on hands on doing and feeling. These are our visual, audio, and kinesthetic learning modalities. In order to reach all of our students, as we teach, we must address the needs of each type of learner by using all three modalities as we present the new material. It is also very interesting to note what brain researchers have documented regarding multiple intelligences that students are born with (social, music, movement, verbal, logic, etc.), and then to incorporate instruction which accommodates these modalities. Be encouraged here as I explain how to do this without having to divide the class by learning modalities and teach the same material in ten different ways.

Let's go back to the three basic learning styles; visual, audio, and kinesthetic. If in every, every, every, every, (hope you got every) class we "told our students, showed our students, and let our students, then we would have reached each learner type. So many teachers just tell or lecture their students, and I believe this is because our most recent instructors were university professors who basically used lecture as their form of instruction. I suggest that we do lecture or "tell" in every presentation, but that we also "show" and "let" in every presentation.

To show means to allow our students to see what we are saying by writing on the marker board or on an overhead projector, or through a power point presentation, or through a demonstration (How about a monologue of President Roosevelt weighing the pros and cons of entering World War II, or a real plant to show the parts of a flower, or actually teaching a phonics class to prospective reading teachers as if they were the first grade students?). Our students have the benefit of more than words when we show and tell.

Finally, for those kinesthetic learners, let's "let" our students actually do something with what they have learned. We have discussed the planets and the order of their positions from the sun. Allow students to represent those planets and the sun and have them rotate around the sun. In math, use manipulatives or have students actually come to the board during the presentation to demonstrate or "do" the steps of solving and then graphing a linear equation. Many times, we do not allow the students to "do" until they have to work independently while doing homework or even a test. "Doing" during the presentation is critical in order for those "hands on" learners to grasp the concepts. Again entire books could be written on each of these modes of presentation, but I believe that you understand and then can create your own "telling", "showing", and "letting" experiences for your students during the presentation.

Regarding multiple intelligence findings that brain research continues to document, I recommend that you incorporate them into the instruction that you give to the entire group. I recently attended a seminar on multiple intelligences in which the presenters advocated that there be learning centers in which each student could learn concepts through his or her most comfortable modality. I like this concept for practice of what is taught, and though one-on-one instruction using each individual student's intelligence would be nice, it is not feasible in most school settings. If we could incorporate music and movement and logic and verbal communication and social interaction and the many other "intelligences" to our instruction, we could reach all of our students without having to give each one a private lesson.

In addition to utilizing the essentials of "telling", "showing", and "letting" during our instruction or presentation, I would also like to emphasize the need for our students to be active participants in their learning and not just receptacles which we put knowledge into. We need to see them as more than just ears, and see ourselves as more than just mouths if you can get this picture. How can our students be active participants? They can participate by taking notes as we speak, here let them utilize their learning modality; outlines for those who are oriented by logic, drawings by those oriented by art, speaking and repeating by the verbally oriented, moving rhythmically by those so oriented, and even singing by those oriented my music. Students can be active by repeating what we just said, or by answering questions over what was just taught, or by summarizing major points at the end of an instructional point. Here again, I would like to strongly recommend that we especially keep those slower students participating and engaged. The point is that our students must be actively engaged while we teach. Most of us teachers love to talk and to demonstrate; that is what teaching is, but we must keep in mind that our students must be active in order to really learn, and we must plan for their active participation even during our instructional time.

Though I believe this point was covered in the chapter regarding preparing to teach, it is worth mentioning again here. We are the teachers; the text book is not. Though many adults and some youth and even children are learning independently through on-line or correspondence courses, I would estimate that at least 80 to 90 percent of learners learn better and prefer a live teacher and the interaction with other students while learning. For this reason, we must not rely on merely having the students read a text book or on us reading the textbook to the students. We must break down that material in a simple way and give our students the essentials in our texts and curriculums until we know they have met the objectives. This is the value of a true teacher. I do not believe that a teacher can or should ever be replaced by a computer or a book. So, once more I emphasize our role during instruction of breaking down the complex and making it simple; taking the whole and showing how each part makes the whole; breaking down complex operations into simple steps, etc...

Finally, I would like to emphasize that during the instruction or presentation of concepts, we should allow time for what I call "guided practice". Guided practice means exactly that; allowing our students to practice while they still have us there to guide them. During instruction, I have given my students information verbally, I have shown them visibly, and I have allowed them to interact with the information or knowledge I have given them. At this point most teachers would send their students to do independent work, and the result would usually be that more than half of the students would raise their hands and ask for additional help or instruction. Since teaching is usually done in groups of fifteen or more, and we do not have the time to offer a private class to so many students, I suggest that we always have students practice as a group with us guiding them before sending them to do independent practice. (Of course there will be that 10% who do not need any guided practice and these should be allowed to proceed.)

Guided practice would be actually allowing the class to tell you what to do as we solve a long division problem together. It is important here not to re-teach by doing the problem for them, but to let them tell you what to do next, and to allow them to do all of the calculations. If you were teaching literature or composition, you would ask them to tell you what the first, second, third and final paragraphs would look like in a two page synopsis of a literary work. In other words, let them practice what you have taught while they still have you as a reference. Doing this will eliminate the frustration that often occurs when students are trying to practice what they have learned, and they have no teacher to remind them of the steps. Guided practice should always be a part of instruction.

In summary, the key to presenting information or instructing our students is to use the three basic learning modalities (verbal, audio, kinesthetic), or put more simply, "tell", "show", and "let". Students must be active participants during instructional time, as being engaged will help them to learn (get information, understand it, and be able to apply what they have learned). Before sending our students to apply independently what we have taught, add some guided practice to the instructional time.

STEP NUMBER FOUR: INDEPENDENT PRACTICE, BECAUSE TRUE LEARNING IS ACTUALLY APPLYING WHAT WAS LEARNED

Now, we are ready to move on to step number four, which will give us an indication of whether our students have truly learned. Remember that true learning includes acquiring knowledge, understanding it, and then having the ability to apply this knowledge (wisdom). In this step, or stage of teaching, our goal is to move our students from prompted, teacher assisted application of what they have learned to independent application of such. I do recommend that this independent practice begin while students are still in the classroom and have the assistance of the teacher, their notes and textbook, and would recommend about ten minutes of in-class practice. Due to limited classroom time, it must continue at home in the form of homework where students have the assistance of their teacher in the form of their class notes and of their textbook, and even of their parents.

The key to independent practice is providing students with many opportunities to actually "do" or apply what we have taught them to do. This practice is an integral part of learning which in recent times has almost become an extinct practice. Understanding our students' and families' busy schedules and life styles, and in order to insure true learning, we must provide our students with ample out of school and class assignments and projects. The objective of these assignments is to allow our students to practice independently and to apply what we have taught them. These assignments should not be rote busy work, but relevant practice assignments of what we have taught them. They can range from doing math problems to master skills, to keeping a journal of literary works read, to creating a model of how the ear works, to creating a budget and system for tracking revenue and expenses for a business, to reading the text regarding a period in history and placing the event and important characters on a time line, etc.. Most curriculum come with ample practice opportunities. As teachers, we must select those activities that will truly help our students to apply and master the concepts that are vital.

Though I have not mentioned this independent practice by the name "homework" thus far, it is mostly exactly that. I suppose this would be a good time to discuss this most dreaded topic of students and even parents; this effort in futility for many teachers. Again, busy schedules, extracurricular activities and classes, distance traveled to and from school and work, the grading required by these assignments, and the trouble getting students to actually do them could cause us to shy away from giving homework and assignments. In order to give our students enough interaction with concepts to acquire mastery and the ability to apply them, we must rely on this out of class independent practice time. Of course students must have time with their family and for other life activities, so we cannot overdo it with homework, but a good amount will be of much learning benefit while still allowing time for other activities.

For an average learner, I recommend a daily time of a good three hours for college students; two hours for upper elementary, junior high, and high school students; and one hour for lower elementary students.

Unfortunately, this concept will not be a popular one for students or parents in most cases, and we will have to teach the value of this independent practice, and also make the assignments rigorous and relevant to learning. Another thing that will help both students and parents in their willingness to participate in independent practice is to give these assignments a week or even a month in advance so that students with the help of their parents can schedule their independent practice assignments around their busy schedules. Posting weekly assignments on the internet (save the trees), or having students copy the assignments on Monday for the entire week (save the trees, and have the assurance that the students really read what they wrote), or handing out printed copies of the assignments at the beginning or end of each week will be helpful.

In addition, we should also remember that independent practice is exactly that, "practice". We must be careful not to take permanent grades over "practice" material such as homework or class work. Of course, we know that in many situations, if something is not going to be graded, students do not always give their full effort, so I suggest grading homework or class work, and giving students the option of correcting the assignments for a "corrected" grade. This system is a great means of re-enforcing learned material, with the great incentive of increasing the homework grade by correcting the items missed. Though most teachers shy away from correcting students' efforts to practice independently (homework, class work), I have found that quickly correcting the "independent practices" in class the following day both re-enforces what a student knows and points out what he does not know. As the student makes the effort to correct those items that he did not know, noting the simple mistake he made or returning to his notes for clarity or even seeking the help of a classmate or teacher, he is involving himself in a very valuable part of the learning process. Allowing grade changes for this effort is a great motivator for most students. In addition, requiring the "correction" process of students scoring below eighty per cent will motivate those who otherwise would be satisfied with where they are at.

Once we have used the six steps to instructing our students so that they will learn (eventually be able to apply what we have taught them, moving from knowledge to understanding to wisdom), then independent practice will become an evaluation or test, with no teacher, notes, textbook, or any other type of assistance. The measure of this knowledge, understanding and wisdom comes in the form of exams while in school, and then the ability to actually do what was learned in true life situations once out of school. A brief caution here: never test over material that has just been taught. Some may protest here in that after teaching the objectives in a particular chapter, a test or exam over the entire chapter must be given. I would suggest that the last parts of that chapter have not had adequate review and practice time and therefore should be put on the next exam.

In summary, independent practice is a vital component of the learning process and when used daily, it will help our students truly master the concepts and objectives we are teaching them. When they are not allowed the opportunity to apply independently what we have taught them, neither they nor we will know whether they have truly learned (have the ability to actually apply) what we have taught them. Now we are ready to move to the fifth step of teaching so that our students really learn. Can you guess what it is?

STEP NUMBER FIVE: REVIEW AGAIN, BECAUSE WE WANT TO INSURE UNDERSTANDING

I heard that! You are saying review, review, review; enough! Because we want to teach so that students really learn, review is a must. This final classroom review time of five minutes or so is just a time to once more re-enforce what we actually taught and learned during this segment of class time. Again, I must stress that review time is not re-teach time. It is very student active, and our role as teachers is to facilitate the discussions amongst students and the interaction of our students with the material which has been taught. It is one more opportunity for us to re-set and re-establish those foundations that we taught before we send our students home to complete the independent practice which we began in class. I will not go into great detail here regarding the review, as the principles we went over in step two will apply here also. Let it suffice to say that this very brief review time is to once more insure that our students have received and understood the concepts we have taught before we send them home to practice independently or to apply these concepts (wisdom).

Part of this very brief final time is to ask our students once more what they learned, i.e. identify once more the community helpers and their roles; have them tell us once more the steps to long division; have them summarize the events leading up to our countries involvement in WWII; have them once more review the writing point of view of a particular author; have them tell us once more what the process of pollination involves; or for our university school of education students, have them list the six steps to teaching that will never fail. The next to the last thing that our students need to leave with should be a synopsis of the essential elements of that day's class. As with everything, the first and last words really stick. Remember how our parents' last words before sending us away to college, or a teacher's last words at the end of a school year, or a speaker or writer's last words stay with you for a long time. Even Jesus took advantage of His last moments with His disciples to review with them the great commission of preaching and teaching the Good News. This was not the first time they had heard about their responsibilities, but He took advantage of the final moments to go over them again. Much can be gained by taking a few moments to give those final "last words" of blessing and commission to our students.

Of course for these final class minutes to be of optimum value, we must plan to stop class before the bell rings or before our time expires. We must avoid the habit of teaching to the last minute and then yelling out the assignment as our students begin the noisy process of exiting our classroom. For those of us who love teaching so much that we forget the time, we must always have control of the dismissal of a class. I always used to tell my students, "The bell does not dismiss you, nor does the time. I dismiss you." Though we always want to respect the time of our students and the fact that they have other classes to attend and other things to do, we should always squeeze in step number five – review or summarize again. As we understand the extreme importance of this next to the last step, we will utilize the last few moments of our class time more effectively.

STEP NUMBER SIX: BLESS, BECAUSE LAST WORDS COUNT AND BECAUSE WE MUST TOUCH OUR STUDENTS' HEARTS IF WE WANT THEM TO ALLOW US THE PRIVILEGE OF BEING THEIR TEACHERS

Now that we have opened class by inspiring and motivating our students; reviewed the previous days' concepts in a dynamic and fun way; taught our students by telling, showing, and letting them; allowed them to begin practicing independently; and permitted them to synthesize today's objectives by reviewing again; we come to the final of the six steps to teaching so that our students truly learn (are able to apply what we have taught).

Step six is to "bless" our students. To bless means to honor; esteem; to bow ones knee to. To bless means to encourage, to inspire, to validate, to compliment, to make our students feel "on top of the world" or to feel "warm and fuzzy inside". They have worked hard this day or this class period. They have been attentive and have disciplined their minds and bodies to stay with us. They have been considerate and respectful of others. They have been interested and engaged. They have thought deeply and brilliantly. In short, they have been a blessing to teach and we sincerely love and appreciate them. Therefore, the very last things that they should hear before they leave are these wonderful words of blessing. As we sincerely express to our students in word or by touch (refer to the elements of the "blessing" in chapter two) our students will wait for, appreciate, and cherish our ending words to them each day. Our words will be like rain falling on dry and parched land, and these words will lift our students up and set our students up for success!

Again, in order to have the time to actually spend one minute or two blessing our students, we will need to stop teaching a few minutes before class is scheduled to end. Standing at the door as they leave and giving each student a hug or hand shake or personal word of encouragement sure beats our yelling out today's assignment or screaming for quiet as they rush to go to the next class or prepare to leave for the day. And by the way, tangible rewards are always welcomed by students of all ages. Rewards do not have to be costly; use your imagination to issue a homework pass, time out pass, early release pass, extra point on a test etc...to bless your students for the outstanding job they do in class. Even a simple treat as they walk out the door is a demonstration of our high esteem for our students, and the higher we esteem them, the higher they will rise.

SUMMARY AND SUGGESTED SCHEDULE

For those who need the steps put into a schedule of time, here is a suggested schedule for a fifty minute class; you can do the math for a thirty minute or a ninety minute class:

Step	% of Class Time	Minutes
Inspiration	5%	2.5
Review	15%	7.5
Instruction	55%	27.5
Independent Practice	10%	5.0
Review	10%	5.0
Blessing	5%	2.5

This is a "suggested" schedule and is not written in stone or even in ink; all things are susceptible to change.

See how easy it is to "eat an elephant" one step at a time? By including these six elements each time we teach our students, I would venture to guarantee a fifty percent chance of students absolutely learning (obtaining the knowledge, understanding, and wisdom – ability to apply what is learned). You might be saying, "Fifty per cent! That is not a very good return rate on all of my effort!" In the next chapter we will discuss an element of teaching which when added to the six easy to remember steps in this chapter, and the principles of chapter two on touching to teach; chapter three on preparing to teach; and chapter four on disciplining to teach; will put us on the road to successful teaching. I get excited at the potential for teaching young people and inspiring them to impact their world, and about accomplishing this awesome task by knowing, understanding and applying (wisdom) the principles set forth in this book! Now, let's move on to chapter six, which we will title "Do It With Pizzazz!".

APPLICATION (WISDOM)

1. *Until the six steps become a habit, (twenty-one class days), write what you will do to "I, R, I, I, R, B" on your lesson plans for every class.*

2. *Each week try a new, fun, dynamic way to review so that it is effective and not boring and redundant.*

3. *Write "Tell Me, Show Me, Let Me" on the first page of your teaching outlines to remind you to use all three modalities and reach all types of learners.*

4. *At least once a week, stand at the classroom door to "bless" each student individually as they leave the classroom.*

5. *Ask students to evaluate your teaching using a scale of one (needs improvement) to four (excellent) at least once a month. Take to heart their comments and continue to change and grow.*

Chapter Six

DO IT WITH PIZZAZZ!

Key Points

1. *Teaching with "Pizzazz" means using everything we have to keep our students awake and engaged as we teach because we cannot teach someone who is asleep.*

2. *We must use our personality (all we have, both internal and external) to gain and retain the attention of our students so that they can learn*

3. *Our method of delivering our subject matter must be memorable and unique, unexpected and captivating, visual and multi-sensory and practiced.*

4. *The curriculum we teach must be both challenging to our students, and proven to be relevant and useful in their current or future lives*

If we were interested in having our students really learn (receive knowledge, understand that knowledge, and apply that knowledge) fifty percent of the time, we could stop reading at chapter five, and be satisfied. Again you might rightfully say, "Fifty percent! No way! I am called to teach and am serious about all of my students learning all of the time." If you are, then I encourage you to continue reading the last five chapters, which are like that very important icing on the cake. Thus far, we have baked a delicious and nutritious cake; we have agreed that teaching is a vocation, a calling that allows us to impact the world by touching the lives of young people; we have acknowledged that we must first touch the hearts of our students before they will give us the privilege of touching their minds and their lives; we have valued the principles of preparing ourselves spiritually and mentally, and of planning both long term and daily; we have understood the principle of authority and good discipline in order to teach our students; and finally, we have learned six basic steps to "really" teaching (Inspire, Review, Instruct, Provide Independent Practice, Review, and Bless). These principles have certainly given us a delicious cake; entire books could be written on each one of the previous topics, and excellent teachers produced by applying those principles, but the frosting would be missing. I like cake, but the frosting is my favorite part. In this chapter entitled "Do It With Pizzazz!", we will learn an important key without which, fifty percent of our students would not learn; this will be like that rich butter and confectioner's sugar icing that we enjoy so much.

"Teaching with Pizzazz" will help us to avoid the greatest complaint of students of all ages and of all times: "This is boring!" When my own children would tell me that they were bored at home, I would always tell them that boredom was a decision, just like happiness. I would tell them to find something to do so that they would not be bored. In the classroom, it is a little different, as our students are actually under lock and key with us, and do not have the freedom to leave or to do something else so that they are not bored. Therefore, I believe that it is our responsibility as teachers to provide a stimulating, rigorous, and even entertaining environment for our students so they will stay awake and be able to learn. In this chapter we will discuss both a rigorous and challenging curriculum, as well as the delivery of that curriculum to our students. Let's begin by taking a hard look at our delivery.

Again, I can hear the protests and the comments. "I am not an entertainer, I am not here to entertain, but to teach!" I strongly believe that actors and teachers have similar personalities. Because teachers do not have all of the sound and visual effects that actors depend on, we really have to rely on personality and on the skills we will learn in this chapter. Some of us might say, "My personality is not outgoing and not entertaining, but I love my subject and I love children; this is why I teach. I do not do flips across the room, yet I strongly desire to be a teacher." There is hope and good news for all of us. Personality is what we are made of as persons. According to Webster, one's personality is the behavioral and emotional characteristics which make us persons. Thank goodness, many things make up who and what we are. That love and strong desire to teach comes from the depth of our beings, and this passion for imparting to others, along with all of the other inner emotions will be very important keys to teaching with pizzazz. In addition, our entire physique, which includes eyes and mouth and hands and feet are an important part of whom and what we are; these parts will also be key to teaching with pizzazz. Add to these the God given ability to create and some skills we can learn on how to deliver our curriculum, and we are on our way to teaching with pizzazz!

PERSONALITY

Let's begin this important topic of gaining and keeping our students' attention in order to truly teach them with a discussion on how we can use our God given personalities to teach. We will deal with both inner and outer aspects of personality. The inner aspects are those things that come from inside of us and move out towards our students. These include our emotions; love, passion, anger, joy, sadness, energy, humor, etc... Though we do not all have outgoing personalities, and some of us might even say that we are not "people people", we all have all of these emotions. We just need to learn the skill of using them as we teach. The other aspect of our personalities is those outer or physical attributes that we have been given, such as everything that is on our face, our appendages, our voice, etc... We can even use the draping of this outer part of us, clothing, make-up, a hat, a mega or micro phone, to our advantage as we teach with pizzazz. Let's learn how to use all that we have been given in order to keep our students awake and engaged and thus truly learning.

PHYSICAL OR OUTER ASPECTS OF PERSONALITY

We will begin with the outer attributes. Look at yourself in the mirror to see the many things that we have been endowed with that can assist us as we communicate with our students. I did say communicate, and true communication must involve both the deliverer and the receiver. Unfortunately in most of our classrooms, only the deliverer is actually active. Can you envision yourself as one big mouth, and your students as huge ears at each of the desks in your classroom? Because we truly want to teach, we must be interested in creating a learning environment in which both teachers and students have both mouths and ears and eyes in order for there to be true communication.

As we look at ourselves in the mirror seeking those external aspects of who we are, let's start at the top and move down. From top to bottom, we find the head first. Without sounding elementary, here we find the forehead, eyebrows, eyes, nose mouth, and even ears. This is also where our vocal chords are located. So, how will we use each of these parts to teach with pizzazz? First, we can all use the face and all that is on it to put some expression into our teaching. Have you ever faced a teacher whose face is set in stone, who never smiles, blinks, or even looks you right in the eye? Of course I am exaggerating a little here, but seriously, we have all had the displeasure of being talked to (I cannot say taught) by this type of teacher. Let's use everything that is on our face to teach with pizzazz. First, let's look our students in the eyes while teaching. When we make eye contact with each one of them, we are not only helping them to focus on what we are teaching, we are telling them that they are important to us; important enough to have us take the time to direct our teaching to them personally. In addition to getting our students' attention and making them feel important with our eyes, we can use our eyes to express excitement, anger, zeal, sadness, joy etc...Add the use of our facial expressions and a great big smile, and we have set an environment for some exciting learning to take place.

The rest of our bodies can also make our teaching dynamic. Since many of our students are strong visual learners, let's use the hands and arms to help demonstrate what we are saying. If it is true that a picture is worth a thousand words, then let's paint pictures with our hands to help our students learn. We can use our legs to move (walk, run, skip, jump) around the room to keep our students actively engaged in what we are teaching. Though it is more comfortable to sit at the desk or stay behind the podium or lectern, walking from side to side and even from front to back while we teach is very valuable in keeping our students alert; just be careful not to rock them to sleep with a slow side to side movement. Jump up on a desk once in a while to re-engage the attention of the class. Even our posture (tall and straight, slumped over, bent forward) can be used to send great messages to our students. And for our more audio learners, let's use our fingers, hands, and even feet to snap, clap, and even stomp making use of rhythm and surprise to help knowledge enter the minds of our now very alert students. As we move about the room, our students also get a little movement as they turn around to see us at the back of the room or look up to find us on top of our desk. Using everything that we have from eyes to feet will wake every sleeping beauty and snoring giant in our classrooms.

Though we may not use everything we have every second, even having an awareness of these tools will make a large difference in our classrooms. In addition to using all that we have, we can also drape what we have to gain attention and interest. How about putting on some black rimmed glasses with a funny nose and a white doctor's coat on days when we will do science experiments or when we want to teach in a very deductive way? Or how about wearing two different shoes one day to get some attention? I once heard of a school where teachers were not allowed to wear red as it was too distracting. I would much prefer for my clothing to attract the attention of my students than for it to bore them! In summary, as we discuss using all of our physical components from facial expressions, to eye contact, to hand and arm movements, to legs and feet, to even the draping of all of this with unusual clothing or props; let's remember to use this equipment to gain and keep the attention of our students so that they can truly learn.

Next, we will discuss another physical attribute that each one of us has regardless of our personality types – the voice. What a great tool for teaching the voice can be! Does our voice add to our teaching, or put our students to sleep? Our voices have many dimensions; volume: loud – soft, pitch: high – low, and rate: fast – slow, so let's utilize a variety of these dimensions to teach with pizzazz. Our students will have to get quiet and strain their ears to hear us when we use a very soft voice to teach. A louder voice gains attention and stresses the importance of a topic. As we vary the pitches of our voice, we eliminate that monotone, which puts our students to sleep. Pitch variations make our teaching exciting, more interesting, and unexpected. Finally, taking full advantage of the rate of our speech; sometimes fast, sometimes very slow, makes our students strain to keep up, push us to move faster, and in general stay engaged. Therefore, let's take full advantage of the ability to speed up or slow down our speech as a tool to gain and keep both attention and interest.

INNER ASPECTS OF PERSONALITY

Now that we have learned how to use everything we have on the outside, let's take a look at the inner aspects of our personality and emotions that will make us dynamic teachers. Great teachers can be extroverts or introverts, and regardless of which we are, we all have the varied aspects of personality which can be turned up or down in the classroom to produce an environment that is electric and active or one that is quiet and pensive, or one that is just boring. First of all, let's consider energy. Granted that some days we have more energy than others, we do have the ability to turn our energy levels up or down. Using high or low energy levels takes our students on an exciting ride of anticipation and culmination in learning. Energy is a dynamo, our high or low level of energy will set the stage for our students' level of interest, effort, and learning. High or low energy and enthusiasm from the source determines the energy for learning of our students, therefore what we put into our teaching will result in what our students put into their learning. And what they put into their learning is what they will get out of their learning. Since this circle begins with us, let's put some "pizzazz" (energy and enthusiasm) into our teaching and get some fantastic results.

In addition to energy, our emotions (love, passion, joy, anger, sadness, fear, etc...) also emanate from our inner beings. The word emotion comes from the French word, "emovoir", which means to "stir up", to move. We have the ability to "stir up" the emotions which we were born with in order to move our students and elicit responses from them. I will never forget addressing a large group of high school students who had poorly represented me and our school when I was out of town. Their response was very calloused until I expressed my sadness and disappointment through actual tears. I was not trying to manipulate them, I was expressing true emotions and even being transparent or real; this caused my students to truly learn the lesson I was teaching; it also caused true repentance, and many apologies. Sometimes it is our expressed passion or zeal or love for what we are teaching that "moves" and inspires our students. Our excitement about what we are teaching is very contagious and raises our students' level of interest and energy. Have you ever noticed what happens when we smile at someone? They usually smile back. We all know that laughter is contagious, and so are the other emotions. Students are naturally motivated by high levels of any of the aforementioned emotions. We can safely break out of society's norm to hide and avoid emotions and use them to our advantage as we teach. A friend of mine (and outstanding teacher) loves teaching English; she expresses that passion and excitement without even thinking by clapping her hands and rubbing them together as she introduces the topic of the day. A History teacher might express some serious anger and sadness when discussing a heated event such as the attack on Pearl Harbor and subsequent bombing of Nakashima.

Our third and fourth internal characteristics, creativity and variety will enlighten and motivate our students to learn. Though some might say that we are not creative, we were all made in the image of the One who created the magnificent universe that we live in. Therefore, we all have the ability to create. As we use our ability to create, we will produce lessons which are interesting and captivating. Our students will never be bored because daily we will seek ways to change and add variety to how we present the universal truths in our lessons, which do not change in a way that is always changing. Someone once said, "All living things are changing; only things that are dead do not change." We must ask ourselves, "Is my teaching dead or alive?" If it is alive, there is variation and change caused by our innate ability to create. There is no limit to the ways of presenting our material to our students. One day we could use a lecture format; another day we could ask questions and have the students research the answers in their books as we go; another day we could have our students work on a project to get the information; another day we could divide our class in two parts and have each present the pro or contra of a topic. There is no limit to the creative and varied ways that we can teach our objectives. We just have to be aware of the need to change daily the way that we present our material to our students.

Though humor could have been discussed above as an emotion, I decided to dedicate a separate paragraph to this very useful classroom tool. Some of you may be like me in that I do not feel that I have a great sense of humor. Generally, others have to explain jokes to me before I get it, and I am by no means witty. Others of you are quite witty and just fun to be around. In spite of the inability to tell jokes and even entertain others, all of us can utilize humor as a tool to keep our classrooms alive if we will just choose to keep the environment light and lively instead of making it heavy and dead. This means that those of us with either no sense of humor or a dry sense of humor will have to laugh at ourselves sometimes, and in so doing, help our students to laugh at themselves too. I am a very serious looking person and consider myself to take everything that I do very seriously, but I have learned to laugh both with my students about myself and about them. We can all tell some great stories of students who said or did the funniest things, or stories of some funny and embarrassing things we said or did. Unfortunately, many of us refused to seize the opportunity to lighten things up a bit by laughing with our students. I remember teaching a seminar in Mexico on the very serious topic of discipline. I was in a small auditorium which had a stage. I do like to take full advantage of my space, and walked from one side of the stage to the other throughout the presentation. Each time I would move to left stage, the teachers would move forward in their chairs and would get a strange, worried look on their faces. I was too busy delivering my presentation to find out why. Half way through the presentation, I realized why. I disappeared (and not so graciously) into a hole that was in the stage! I could have jumped right back out and continued, but instead I chose to be real and laugh with my students about myself. I know that I will never forget that day or what I was teaching and to whom. I know that the teachers there will not forget that day or the topic either. As we allow humor in our classrooms, and laugh both with and at our students and ourselves, we show our students that we are transparent and real, and even vulnerable or open. This in turn creates an open and receptive environment for learning. Some of us need to purpose to add some laughter and humor each day (even write it into our lesson plans in green or orange). Accomplishing this may involve going on the internet or buying a book of funny riddles or jokes. I have noticed that some of the most captivating speakers warm up their audiences with a couple of jokes at the beginning of their discussions.

In summary, we can use everything that we have to keep our students awake and engaged; this everything means both the outward physical things from our faces and everything that is on them, to our hands and arms and legs, as well as our inner qualities such as emotions, creativity, humor and transparency. We really have quite a collection of internal and external tools to use so that our students will never accuse us of being boring. Let's add a couple of skills to these handy tools, and we will be teaching with pizzazz. Who knows, we might even enjoy teaching as much as our students enjoy our teaching.

VARIETY

To wrap up this chapter, let's discuss some techniques or skills that will add pizzazz to our classrooms. We briefly mentioned the first one when we discussed our innate ability to create and produce variety or change. We want to have classrooms that are alive, therefore, that lesson that we wrote during our first year of teaching five years ago needs to be changed; it is stale and outdated. Those overheads that we produced need to be updated and even converted to a power point presentation. We can jump on the internet and visit a virtual classroom, or foreign country or even interact with students in a nation which we are currently studying. Though students require structure and consistency regarding schedules and procedures, they appreciate and learn more when we vary our methods of instruction from day to day and from class to class and even from time block to time block. We can begin class by asking numerous questions about what we will teach; then ask if anyone is really interested in finding the answers to these questions; and even let our students research the answers during class. We can use a combination of lecture and questioning. We can use role play (usually monologues or even dialogues as we play two parts). We can have discussions, and debates, and dramas, and demonstrations, and experiments, and there is no limit to the different ways that we can present material. We can teach through projects and group activities. Our objectives do not change, but when we vary our delivery methods, our students will actually look forward to the next class just to see what new and creative delivery method we will use! Because they are interested, they will learn more and love learning! And all of these delivery variations can be learned and tried; we do not have to have outgoing or entertaining personalities; we just have to desire to teach with pizzazz by putting a little spice in it. Variation is the spice of teaching. Our students too would appreciate a little or a lot of spice as they try to "eat that elephant" one bite at a time.

STYLE – THE PROCESS BY WHICH WE DELIVER OUR SUBJECT MATTER

If variety is the spice of our teaching, then style is the icing. We will define "style" as the process by which we deliver our subject matter (Wilkinson, 2000).

The greatest teacher on the earth, Jesus Christ used incredible style as he taught and literally revolutionized the world in just three years of full time teaching. We remember and continue to apply the teachings that God gave us in the Bible due to His "Style". According to Wilkinson, Jesus used seven style techniques: memorable, unexpected, visual, unique, multisensory, captivating, and practiced (Wilkinson, 2000). I will briefly explain each of these techniques, and highly recommend that you take the seminar or purchase the DVD's of this course. Though the course was designed for Sunday school teachers, any teacher can benefit from it. If we consistently use these elements in our teaching, our students will not only learn, understand, and apply what we teach, they will never forget it!

MEMORABLE AND UNIQUE

Who could forget a fiery inferno heated seven times hotter than normal, or a man in the belly of a whale, or a boy's lunch feeding multitudes. Through these memorable illustrations, we also still remember God's teaching objectives of Divine protection, the need for obedience to God, and His supernatural provision. When we attach our objective to something memorable, we drastically improve the chances that our students will retain what we have taught. Here are some examples of objectives and memorable illustrations that we could use (some may be ones you have already used). In math, greater than and less than signs; make your arms the mouth of an alligator that when deciding on dinner always chooses the largest amount. In English, use students performing actions or having actions performed on them to illustrate active and passive voice, and the benefits to using the active voice when writing. In History, turn off the lights and actually ride a stick horse through the classroom announcing, "The British are coming!" In Science, show the video "The Silent Scream" before discussing the development stages of a human baby. When teaching on "exceptional children" and their characteristics and learning styles, grill and drill one of the teachers in the room for a couple of minutes. No matter what we teach, we can use memorable illustrations that will not only help our students understand the information we teach, but that will also tie it to something that they can easily retrieve from their memories.

UNEXPECTED AND CAPTIVATING

Using the unexpected will also help our students to comprehend and retain information. It will certainly captivate our students' attention. Again using the style of God to illustrate this point, who would expect a donkey to speak, or water to flow from a rock, or for a Man to walk on water? And we must certainly agree that the attention of many was captivated through these unexpected events. And even today, it is easy for us to recall the lessons learned from these unexpected illustrations (God's instructions, His provision, and His supernatural ability). Our use of the unexpected to captivate our students' attention will likewise help our students to learn and recall our teaching objectives. I know that the readers of this book are teachers of many subjects, and of students of many grade levels and ages, thus examples from many disciplines and grade levels. Our college biology students would not expect to find a live monkey in the classroom as we discuss the truth or fallacy of evolution; nor would our high school trigonometry students expect to determine the length and width of an awning which would shade the playground in the afternoon through the use of the Pythagorean theory. How about "unexpected guests" as kindergarteners study community helpers, or holding a sixth grade science class outside to discover and even gather specimens of ferns or conifers or gymnosperms or other types of trees? Again, there is no limit to finding unexpected ways to cement our content into the memories of our students; the key is to remember the value of the unexpected in our teaching.

VISUAL AND MULTISENSORY

Due to the great technological advances of media, we have become very much visual learners. Years ago, music was listened to; today, it is both listened to and watched. Before television, stories were listened to on the radio; today they are watched and even felt through amazing advances in sound technology. Yet our teaching for the most part relies on hearing our voices and to a small degree seeing what little we write on the board or an overhead. We have the exciting and amazing ability to enhance our instruction by taking advantage of all of the major technological advances. A computer, an "LCD" projector, and the internet enable us to transport our students to any place in the world. It allows us to bring into our classrooms infinite visuals on any topic we can imagine! By using an internet site and a projector, we can actually take our classes on a virtual tour through some of the great forests, through some of the greatest museums, or even travel through the blood stream to the organs of the human body. Instead of just looking at text book pictures or renditions of human anatomy or of cities in the world, why not take a "virtual tour" through the internet. With this great technology, without even leaving their classroom our students could experience the American Revolution through the writings and artifacts of Thomas

Jefferson which are held in the Library of Congress (try this site: www.loc.gov/exhibts/treasures/trm035.html)!

In addition to audio and visual presentations, let's incorporate all of the senses in our presentations to include touch and taste and even smell. When studying Botany and specifically flowering plants, why not bring in actual flowers to demonstrate the differences between monocots and dicots, and allow our students to use all of the senses as they study what can sometimes be a very boring topic? Why not allow our students to understand acids and bases by letting them use the sense of taste verses telling them and asking them to memorize lists of the two. It has been proven that manipulatives (items to touch and feel) are vital when first introducing mathematical concepts. And how about the use of smell when discussing environmental issues? Or, how about a dramatic reading of a section of the "Scarlet Letter" to put tears in the eyes of the students or "goose bumps" on their skins?

The point here, is to incorporate as many of the senses as possible in order to reach all of our students. Not only does this make material more readily understood, it also makes material more memorable, and it makes the classroom more interesting and learning more exciting.

PRACTICED

The last element of what we are calling "style" or the way in which we deliver our subject matter is "practiced". Put very simply and using an idiom that is highly overused, "Practice what you preach." Today's students and probably the students of every generation are looking for "real" people, who actually do what they teach others to do. If we are teaching our students to have respect for people in authority such as police officers, government officials, and parents, then they must see our example. We will not speak negatively about our own parents, principal, President etc..., unless we desire for those whom we teach to do the same. We cannot be people of "Do what I say, not what I do." If we teach a certain methodology and format for solving an equation, then we ourselves must practice that procedure if we want our students to do the same. We want our students to hear and heed what we are saying, unhindered by the loudness of what we are doing. They will follow our examples – good or bad, not necessarily our words. I suppose that this last element is more than a skill, it is a character trait, which of course must come from the inside. Because we desire to "really teach" our students, we must make a decision to be "doers" or "models" of what we teach. This sounds a little "preachy", but I feel it is a necessary part of having students that are tuned in and engaged with what we teach. Students are quick to discern a fake from the real thing, and will heed instruction or not based on this one issue. Therefore, practice what you preach or teach, do what you ask others to do, and be who you say they are supposed to be.

I believe that every day of every class should bring with it at least one of the above mentioned elements of style. Why, because no one can teach students who are not engaged, or students who are bored, or even worse, students who are asleep, and those of us who teach because it is our vocation, not our job are seriously interested in teaching so that our students acquire knowledge, understand it, and ultimately apply it.

RIGOROUS AND RELEVANT CURRICULUM FOR PIZZAZZ

In addition to using all we have and to using "style" as we teach, we must teach curriculum that is both rigorous and relevant. Most teachers do not have the option of selecting their own curriculum, but I do believe that it is time for us to get involved in curriculum review and selection committees! Who knows more what students need to know than the teachers who teach those subjects year after year. If our curriculum is not of itself academically challenging, then let's supplement it! If our curriculum does not demonstrate how our students will use what they are learning in real life, then let's show them its relevancy!

Personally, I get very concerned to see that year after year our text books are "dumbed down" and to see that year after year our students and our education in the U.S. ranks lower and lower when compared to that of other countries. It takes challenging and relevant curriculum to get the interest and attention of our students. Our students are so capable and can learn so much more than we are asking of them! I have four children, and taught the first one to read and count and add by age four. He went to kindergarten at age five and hated school because it was no challenge for him. I hesitated to teach my three daughters too much for fear that they too would be bored by an unchallenging curriculum. If our curriculum was stronger then we would not have to be teaching to the state written tests, and we could return to using nationally administered standardized achievement testing to measure the accomplishments of our students.

Curriculum does exist that actually makes what is learned relevant to real life! (I love the Glencoe High School Math Curriculum.) Our students must know how they will actually use what they are learning to function in society! How many times do we hear our students ask, "When am I ever going to use this?" Relevant and rigorous curriculum along with great (not good) teachers and parents who participate in their children's educations will motivate our students to learning once more!

When we add the elements of what I call "Pizzazz" to our teaching, we increase the chances of our students really learning. What were those elements? The first was personality which included both our internal elements such as emotion, joy, passion, etc... and the external physical attributes that we all possess (eyes, voice, hands, feet, etc...). To this, we add "style" (the method we use to deliver our subject matter). Here, we discussed delivery modalities that included: Memorable and Unique, Unexpected and Captivating, Visual and Multisensory, and Practiced. Add the third component of rigorous and relevant curriculum and we will be teaching with such "Pizzazz" that our students will not complain of being bored. By incorporating one or more of these techniques in our daily teaching, we are sure to reach a greater percentage if not a full one hundred per cent of our students each day. Wow! What a concept! Incorporating the philosophies and strategies and techniques and skills discussed thus far would revolutionize our teaching and make every student (almost?) love school and learning, but for those who still want more, read on. In the next four chapters, we will add decorations to that icing on the cake. We will discuss the practical uses of brain research; we will discuss those "exceptional" students; we will talk about guarding our students through proper supervision, and finally we will discover one of the greatest teaching assets – our students' parents.

APPLICATION (WISDOM)

1. *Every week make a decision to try using one physical attribute (voice, facial expression, hands, feet, etc... and one internal attribute (joy, humor, anger, etc...) to keep your students' attention; use a symbol and write it on your lesson plan to remind you to use it.*

2. *Add at least one delivery change to your instruction every week in at least one class.*

3. *Add one new delivery method to your lesson plans each week.*

4. *Compare and supplement your curriculum to one used in a private or college preparatory school.*

5. *Demonstrate to your students how every concept you teach will be used in real life.*

6. *After one month, hand out rating cards with the numbers five (boring) through ten (outstanding, dynamic) on them. Have them hold up their cards and average your rating. If you are really brave allow them to do this on a daily basis.*

Chapter Seven

BRAIN RESEARCH MADE PRACTICAL

Key Points

1. *Emotional security and well-being give our students optimal brain functioning.*

2. *Oxygen, proper nutrition and sufficient sleep produce strong brain activity.*

3. *The brain latches on to knowledge which is connected with previously learned concepts.*

4. *Music, rhythm and movement enhance our ability to learn.*

5. *There are at least seven learning modalities (Multiple Intelligences), which can be utilized to help every student learn easier: verbal, logical, visual, musical, body, interpersonal, and intrapersonal.*

6. *The "Primacy-Recency Effect" (PT1, DT, and PT2) helps us use optimal learning times within a class period to teach important concepts.*

Before we dive in to this very intriguing and interesting topic, let's re-affirm some of the principles and skills which we have already learned. Teaching is such a very vital and rewarding vocation (not profession or job) because it enables us to mold and train individuals who will impact the world. Our students actually make a decision to allow us to teach them; therefore we must first touch their hearts before they will allow us to reach their minds. If we fail to prepare, then we have planned to fail. If we cannot control our students then we cannot teach them, so we use the principle of authority and instruction, words, rewards, consequences, organization and dynamic teaching to create an environment in which all of our students can learn. We use the six steps of "one bite at a time" techniques so our students really learn and retain what they learn. And finally, we teach with "Pizzazz" in order to keep our students awake and engaged. All of this makes up a very solid foundation and even the walls and roof of our educational construction. The following chapters will serve to add those wonderful details that will make our teaching even more effective as we strive to be great and not just good teachers.

Let's begin this chapter with a major disclaimer: I am no expert in the field of brain research! Nevertheless, I do find the brain research conclusions fascinating and very helpful to educators as we attempt to teach students with the most effective techniques and learning environments possible. In this chapter we will discuss what I feel are some of the most helpful and applicable to the classroom brain research concepts. Without necessarily being experts in the field of brain research, we will review and discuss ways to actually apply these important findings as we attempt to "really teach" our students.

The recent studies on the brain and how it functions and how all of this research relates to education and learning are so captivating and interesting! The studies on this topic inspire us and also confirm some of the things that we already knew about teaching as they relate to brain functioning. In this chapter, we will attempt to make brain research simple to understand, and very practical so that we can use this vast knowledge and wisdom to help our students not only learn better, but retain what they learn. The language and simplicity of this discussion would probably insult the researchers, but will help the classroom teacher use the findings to assist every learner in his quest for wisdom (the application of what we learn). Many of us have read the research and even attended seminars and conferences regarding the implications of brain research on education, but unfortunately, there has been little teaching on how to actually use the findings in a practical way to enhance learning in the classroom. This will be the purpose of this short chapter. The emphasis of our review and discussion will be the research that connects effective learning with emotional well-being; oxygen, nutrition and rest; learning contexts; music, rhythm, and movement; multiple intelligences; and primacy recency effect.

EMOTIONS AND OPTIMAL BRAIN ACTIVITY

We will begin our discussion with the all important consideration of an individual's emotions as they attempt to learn. The emotional state of our students will either stimulate or impede the brain's functioning. The research is showing us that our emotions can either enhance or hinder our learning. Negative emotions such as stress or fear can short circuit the brain's normal functioning, while positive emotions such as joy and peace can enhance its functioning. Our students will learn and perform better when they are emotionally stable; when they know that "all is well" and they are accepted and loved. It is rather difficult for a student to learn when he or she is afraid, insecure, angry, or in general concerned about what just happened in the car on the way to school or about what just happened in the hall right before class. Though to some of us this may sound like way too much, our classroom must become a "haven" so to speak where our students are protected and re-assured and where there is a general sense of "all is well". It is no wonder that a pre-school student cries on the first day or week or even month of school when all of a sudden they are left with complete strangers in an environment which is completely foreign to the familiar environment of their home. And how much learning actually takes place in the midst of the fear and anxiety of this foreign environment called school. It might be more effective to have parents bringing those children to school for a few five minute visits just to meet and familiarize them with their teacher and environment before school actually starts. This same scenario can be true not only of younger learners, but also in regards to teen learners or even adult learn-ers. No matter who we teach, emotional well-being will be a pre-requisite of full brain functioning and learning. Obviously, we cannot solve all of our students' problems, but we can help our students to be aware of their emotions and how they affect their learning. In addition, we can help them to understand, acknowledge and express these emotions in positive ways. Finally, we can help our students to learn to put the emotions and causes of them aside for a few moments while we attempt to teach them, and while they attempt to learn something.

In a previous chapter we discussed beginning each class with a time of "inspiration". As we invest the first two to five minutes inspiring and motivating and even putting our students concerns outside the classroom door, we will reap the benefits of much more effective learning time. In addition to this type of motivational beginning, which may even include a joke and some encouraging words, we can also make our classrooms safe places for learning where students and teachers accept and respect individuals with their unique personalities and opinions and responses. I know that what I am describing may seem very idealistic and almost utopian, but I do believe that this environment is totally possible as we teachers set the standard to accept each and every student in spite of the diversity of learning style or personality type, or even cultural or racial background. Our students will follow our lead as we welcome and honor each and every student; the quick and slow to respond, the disciplined and not so disciplined, the confident and not so confident. We should always encourage our students to be kind and patient in their comments and attitudes towards one another.

In addition to creating and maintaining the above mentioned atmosphere, let's share some practical ways of helping our students get into "emotional condition" to learn. We must definitely utilize the "inspiration" time of our classroom to share an encouraging story, speak encouraging words, quote an uplifting verse, or even tell a funny joke. In addition, let's be mindful of and watchful for those students who seem perturbed, unhappy, angry, or any other hindering emotion. We could ask them if they need to talk and even have a trustworthy classmate talk with them for a few moments outside while we get started with class. We can also teach our students to "put the problem on hold" for fifty minutes since we will not be able to solve it during class time anyway. In general, we should either deal with the negative emotion and its cause or divert both to a later time (after class or even after school) when we or someone else can help them solve the problem creating the impeding emotion.

In summary, before we can address the academic needs of our students effectively, the emotional security needs of our students must first be met. The brain will not even begin to function until this need is met. We have all studied Maslow's hierarchy of needs, and can note that after the physical needs are met; security, love, and esteem are required before learning can take place. Therefore, we will re-emphasize the fact that the brain will not fully function until the basic need for security and acceptance is met. Next we will deal with the physical needs that must be met in order for the brain to function optimally.

THE VALUE OF OXYGEN, NUTRITION, AND REST FOR OPTIMAL LEARNING

Over and over brain research connects healthy brains with optimal learning. The findings concur with what is very obvious to us regarding the needs of the brain. The brain must have oxygen, proper nutrition and proper rest or sleep in order to be healthy. When any of these three elements are lacking, studies show that the brain will not perform at optimal levels. It is for this reason that free meals are provided in schools for underprivileged students. Of course, the nutritional value of these meals has been challenged, but the principle is a correct one – poor or no nutrition means low functioning. It is also for this reason that fitness in schools must still be a priority. And finally, it is for this reason that we are hearing so much regarding sleeping disorders and the results of poor sleep on functioning. Though insuring that our students' health is at maximum is really the responsibility of their parents, as teachers, we can help to educate our parents and students on the important research findings that note the importance of oxygen, nutrition,

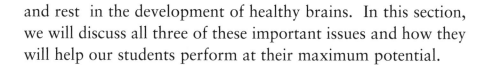

and rest in the development of healthy brains. In this section, we will discuss all three of these important issues and how they will help our students perform at their maximum potential.

OXYGEN FOR OPTIMAL FUNCTIONING

Let's begin our discussion with the brain's need for oxygen in order to function. We all know that without a sufficient supply of oxygen, our bodies shut down completely. This is why stroke, heart attack, and even accident victims are put on oxygen immediately after a life threatening incident. Without oxygen the brain dies, this is why the breathing tubes are inserted and eventually removed to save a life or to end a life. This is why if the cabin of an airplane loses pressure, those handy oxygen masks drop down. Not only do we need oxygen to live, recent studies have proven that our brains actually function better when "oxygenized". The point here is that we must have plenty of oxygen. And what are the two best sources of oxygen other than a direct connection to a tank? Exercise and water.

We will begin our discussion with water. The human body is made of two-thirds water; and the human brain is estimated to be made of 90% water. Therefore, it is important to keep it well hydrated because water helps the blood deliver both oxygen and nutrients to the different parts of the body. Doctors recommend at least 8 glasses (two liters) of water per day as we lose 250 ml daily just by breathing! Of course we should increase intake based upon physical activity and the climate we live in. They also suggest that we not depend upon other forms of liquids such as soft drinks or even sports drinks to reach our minimum intake of water due to their high content of diuretics and even salt. Regarding water and learning, it is obvious that proper hydration will affect learning in a positive way.

Drinking water both before and during class will increase concentration and even performance. We all know that stress causes perspiration and even dehydration, and the lack of concentration. Drinking water before and during a stressful situation like a test can actually improve concentration. Simply put, and so easily done, add the consumption of plenty of water to the learning environment, and we have added brain power and concentration also! Investing in a filtered water apparatus for our classrooms will make a lot of difference in the functioning of our students. In lieu of this, ask every student to daily bring to school a two liter plastic container filled with filtered water. Unfortunately, most people do not like water, but whatever we begin to ingest, we begin to desire, and so it will not be long before our students acquire a "taste" for water. Of course, with the intake of more water, our students will require more restroom breaks; also not a problem as this will give them that much needed movement as they quickly take these breaks and return to the classroom ready to learn more.

If water is an excellent source of oxygen for the brain, then it is logical that exercise will be another important source of oxygen for the brain. When we exercise, we intake greater amounts of oxygen; this in turn causes our brains to function at optimal levels. Studies have shown that students perform at optimal levels right after their physical education class. Other research indicates that aerobic fitness and pulmonary function are predictive of cognitive performance and speed of processing, which underlies performance on a majority of cognitive tasks. There is much research to be studied, but I want to keep this very simple and in "laymen" terms. Nevertheless, I strongly believe that one of the best ways to help our students perform at optimal levels is to allow them some quick, but rigorous physical activity before a challenging mental task. Taking a two minute break to move or jump, or placing some of the most difficult classes or tasks right after PE class will enhance the brain functioning of our students and thus improve their performance. Again, we might argue that we do not have enough time as it is to teach our subject, but time spent increasing the oxygen flow to the brain through physical activity will be worth every minute invested in this manner. I encourage you to try some calisthenics before a difficult test, or to take a "movement" break while teaching a difficult concept. You will notice increased attention and performance.

NUTRITION

Now that we are convinced of the benefits of increased oxygen through consumption of water and through physical activity, let's discuss briefly and simply the need for proper nutrition. Remember how our mothers always said that we should eat a good breakfast every day? They were absolutely right when it comes to having brains that are ready to perform mental tasks. Unfortunately most students go to school each morning either without having eaten breakfast, or after having eaten a breakfast that is loaded with processed sugars (most cereals, pancakes with syrup, a Danish, etc...). Without getting too technical, the brain's favorite food is glucose. Ah, you might say, glucose, sugar, candy, yummy! Wrong! Consuming fruit loops, a fructose filled granola bar, a candy bar or even sweetened chocolate milk right before mental activity, contrary to common belief, may not stimulate the brain strongly enough or for the needed duration of time necessary to perform tough mental functions. Consumption of processed sugars and carbohydrates gives the brain a quick rise and then a sudden crash right when we are in the middle of our intense mental activity.

This will not work. Where does the brain get its glucose from? The most efficient way is through natural sugars such as fruits and many vegetables and through complex carbohydrates. So instead of that breakfast or lunch filled with processed foods high in processed sugar, how about one that includes some fruit, some sort of grain (wheat bread, oatmeal, etc...), and even some eggs or yogurt. I do not claim to be a nutritionist, but common sense tells me that a lunch which includes a soft drink, peanut butter and jelly sandwich, "Twinkies" and potato chips will not provide the brain or the body for that matter with the nutrition necessary to perform at optimal levels. Again, you may right-fully point out that we have no control or even responsibility over what our students eat, but we can certainly help our parents and students understand the value of good "brain food" for healthy learners. In addition, our students need to have nutrition often. Early childhood regulations require children from birth to four years old to eat about every two to three hours. Therefore in addition to their main meals, these children are given snacks between meals. I believe that this principle should not be neglected as our students go into elementary, high, and even post-secondary school. We want to encourage our students to eat a healthy breakfast and lunch, and in addi-tion, to have some healthy snacks between and after these meals. Understanding that this may be a difficult campaign to implement, the value of it would make it a worthwhile endeavor. Just like in kindergarten, students could take turns bringing in snacks for the entire class. They should be healthy and non-processed snacks such as fruit, nuts, veggie's, etc... Another solution would be for each student to bring his or her own mid-morning and afternoon snack along with their lunch on a daily basis. Another solution would be for the school cafe-teria or another school organization to sell healthy snacks.

Again, sometimes this can be a losing battle as our students are addicted to high sugar snacks, and when you put a fruit vending machine next to a candy or chip machine, the fruit machine usually goes bankrupt. Still, based on the knowledge that we now have regarding high brain functioning and nutrition, we certainly can and should educate and encourage our students and parents along these lines. Enough said, as teachers who desire optimal results, let's jump on the cause of proper and frequent nutrition for our students.

REST FOR OPTIMAL BRAIN FUNCTIONING

Lastly, and hopefully briefly, I would like for us to consider the need for proper rest in order for our brains to function properly. I will not begin to site the research studies and statistics regarding sleep deprivation and brain functioning in order to keep my word on making this book easily understood and practical, but I must say that study after study validates this point. During sleep, our bodies are able to perform the maintenance and repairs that cannot be done while the "engine" is running. A mechanic always turns off the engine before doing any and all repairs on a vehicle. For humans, sleep time is crucial for this maintenance and for the necessary repairs. The brain takes our sleep and rest time to file and organize the data, thoughts, and concepts of the day. This is the time when items in our short term memory are placed in long term memory in such an organized way that we are able to recall the information and put it into practical use. Remember nap time in kindergarten and even during infancy? Because so much learning and growth is occurring, plenty of sleep time is also necessary. Even though college and high school students would love the luxury of "nap time", it is of course not feasible, but enough sleep is an essential component of true learning. Once more, what control do we as educators have over this aspect of our students' lives? I insist that as educators, we have much influence over our students. Giving our students and their parents an awareness of these concepts, and then re-emphasizing or reviewing them will make a great amount of difference in the choices and actions of our students. We may be quite surprised, and I encourage us to make the effort and enjoy the fruit of this effort to promote brilliant students with alert and sharp minds through encouraging our students to get a lot of oxygen through exercise and drinking plenty of water, through practicing wise nutrition, and by getting sufficient sleep.

Now that we have dealt with the brain's basic physical and emotional needs, let's discuss its natural tendency to attach new information to previously learned material.

THE BRAIN LATCHES ON TO KNOWLEDGE TAUGHT IN CERTAIN CONTEXTS

Research points out that the bran embraces or accepts new knowledge more readily when it can be "latched on to," "connected to," or related to previous knowledge or experiences. Since the brain has already "filed" the previous information in long term memory, it is easier for the new information, which is now connected to previously learned information to be handled (filed and then retrieved) by the brain. We are using this important research finding when we begin each day by reviewing previously taught information and by using this previously taught information to lead in to today's discussion topic. And when we begin a new topic, we will set the stage for more efficient learning by tying our introduction back to a previously learned concept or experience. In addition, as we connect the concepts taught in each lesson and in turn show how they relate to a whole unit or chapter, the brain will systematically organize and file these jointed blocks of knowledge and our students will be able to apply the knowledge to real situations. Our lessons must not be separate islands, but must be like puzzle pieces which make a whole picture. To do this, we can either go from the larger picture to the individual pieces, or we can show how the individual pieces are building the larger picture.

My youngest daughter was taking a humanities course which is the study of aspects of the human condition. This class includes the arts, literature, history, communication and other disciplines. Though my daughter is a very conscientious and diligent student, there seemed to be a major struggle before during and after each exam. Somehow, the material seemed to be hundreds and hundreds of separate pieces of information and therefore it was very difficult to find the hours and hours of time to study. We suggested that she connect the events and characters and details either by chronological time or by civilization and culture. The use of this technique to build our information bank will help our students to both acquire and understand knowledge, and then apply that knowledge in the form of higher level thinking regarding it.

Another example would be to review addition and how it works and then attach the concept of subtraction to those concepts. Reviewing the skeletal system and attaching the knowledge on the muscular system to this previously learned concept will assist in learning it. Then tying all of the systems together will help the brain to organize, classify, file, retain, and utilize this myriad of information. Attach, attach, attach is the key to applying this principle. Now that we have taught our five year olds the short vowel sounds we will attach in the same way the initial sounds of the consonants; then put them together to form a blend and then a word!

Demonstrating the relevance of what we are teaching is another effective way to use this "latching on" principle. We are constantly bombarded with a lot of irrelevant material, and our bran naturally discards this type of data, but if we demonstrate or share the relevance of what we are teaching with our students the brain will "latch on" to this material. We have all heard our students ask if this material is going to be on the test, or ask why we even have to study certain things. They do not see the relevance of what we are teaching and therefore do not learn the material. When we explain how this material will be used in "real life", or when we state that it will indeed be on the next test, students then actively engage with the material. If we do not show them or convince them of the relevance and utilization or application of what we are teaching, then they will not engage. Many students have difficulty learning Algebra because they never get a sense of how helpful it is when we are missing numbers in real life. If we can show them we can find missing numbers by calling this missing number a letter and then using the algebra rules to solve this "equation", then it will become relevant and worth learning. We must show the relevance of everything we teach. At this point, we may be questioning the relevance of some of the things we teach, and to this I say, if it is not relevant, then let's get rid of this information pollution to the brain, and let's major on those concepts that are truly valuable to and usable by our students. To summarize, connecting previous experiences and knowledge and stating and demonstrating the relevance of what we are teaching will help our students to learn the material we are presenting today. Now let's move on to another fascinating finding that will help material enter the brains of our students.

MUSIC, RHYTHM AND MOVEMENT

Brain research has proven that using movement, music and rhythm also helps our students to learn. It is amazing how we can still remember the words to songs that we learned when we were children or teenagers. No matter how many years have passed, when we hear the tune, we can sing every single word. When I am looking for a Book of the Bible, I still find it by singing the books of the Bible song I taught my fifth/sixth grade students. The research has proven that music improves cognition, stimulates emotion, relieves stress, and enhances memory. Because this is true, music is a very valuable tool in helping our students learn. We can use it to set the stage for enhanced learning in our classroom by playing it as our students enter the classroom and while they are working independently. We can learn those many important facts more easily by setting them to music. We can inspire and challenge our students as they study a difficult math topic, with a very lively and exuberant piece of music, or use a very sad piece of music to move our students to emotions which will cause them to learn about the tragedy and graveness of war. We can play music during an exam to relieve stress and enhance the memory of our students. Using a lap top, the internet, and some very inexpensive speakers, we can take advantage of volumes of musical tunes downloadable and playable at no cost with the press of a few keys. For years parents have been asking their teens to "turn off the music" while they study; it might just be that students have known this very effective way to enhance learning for a long time. Let's take advantage of this valuable tool as we endeavor to help our students learn and perform at their highest level of cognition. By the way cognition is the storage and recall of information (I promised to keep this book non-technical).

And what happens to most people when they hear music or a particular rhythm or beat? It is as if we were programmed to appreciate and know what to do when we hear rhythm or music. Even a child who has not been taught to dance or move to music intuitively moves his body to the sound of music. Research has shown us that those individuals who study a musical instrument early in life do much better in academic learning later in life. Music, rhythm and movement seem to extend and expand the brain's ability for further learning. If this is true, and researchers believe that it is, then we should strive to make music and rhythm and movement an integral part of every pre-school (at home or in school) program, and all three should also be incorporated into the learning process of students of all ages and of all disciplines of study. Not only do music, rhythm, and movement help to get knowledge into our students more easily, they can also be used to help our brains function at optimum levels. When we move, our circulation improves taking more oxygen to the brain and nutrients to all of the cells in our bodies. This of course adds to our overall well-being, and especially helps our brains to function optimally. Taking some "movement" breaks in the form of standing, stretching, or even doing some calisthenics or simple movement gives the brain a break in which to organize and process information. After sitting for twenty or more minutes, blood tends to pool in the seat and in the feet. By standing for only 45 seconds, we will increase the blood flow to the brain by 15% (Glenn, 2002). Standing and exercising relieves the spinal cord and allows for a better flow of spinal fluid. Add music and rhythm to these breaks, and those brain highways become super freeways!

Let's share some practical examples of using music, rhythm and movement to enhance learning. Anything that needs to be memorized can be put to a familiar tune. For example, if we need to learn all the states and their capitols, let's sing them from west to east to "Oh My Darling Clementine" (Anchorage, Alaska; Spokane, Washington; Portland, Oregon; etc...). We can clap between the syllables of spelling words, and snap and clap and bend as we say our multiplication tables (7 x 7 ; 49 snap, clap, jump, or dip 49 snap, clap, jump, or dip). To settle our students' emotions, have nice calming music on as they enter the classroom. Play invigorating music while they have small group discussions over controversial topics. Again, we can use our imaginations. The point is to incorporate music, rhythm and movement into our teaching to enhance learning. Now not all of our students will want to "shake a leg" or "do a little turn", but moving while learning will be a life saver for many of our students. This brings me to our next important research finding – that of multiple intelligence or diverse learning styles.

MULTIPLE INTELLIGENCE RESEARCH AND PRACTICAL CLASSROOM IMPLEMENTATIONS

In addition to helping us understand the value of setting the emotional levels of our students on "comfortable"; increasing brain functioning through proper "oxygenation", nutrition, and rest; "tying" new material to previously learned material; and using music, rhythm, and movement to enhance learning; I would like to discuss briefly the research findings of Howard Gardner and others regarding Multiple Intelligences. Put simply, different people learn better in different contexts due to the fact that they have stronger intelligence in different areas. Gardner initially suggested that there are seven basic "intelligences", which I like to call learning aptitudes and learning styles:

↳ Verbal (Students who learn best with words verbal and written)

↳ Logical (Students who learn best when questioned and required to think logically)

↳ Visual (Students who learn best when they can see what is being taught)

↳ Musical (Students who excel in and can learn best when knowledge comes through music and rhythm)

↳ Body (Students who learn best when movement and knowledge are put together)

↳ Interpersonal (Students who learn best in groups and through interaction with others)

↳ Intrapersonal (Students who learn best independently, without the constant aid of a teacher or other students)

I have explained each "intelligence" very simply, and we can probably agree that these findings are not new to educators. I would caution here that no student learns in just one of these modalities, and that no student functions in only one of these intelligences. Most of us, though we did not call these learning styles or aptitudes "intelligences," were aware that some students had strengths in certain areas, and learned best in these learning contexts. Though we have engaged in many discussions and read much literature regarding multiple intelligences, even Gardner admits that we have failed to use this information to improve instruction. I have also observed a gambit of teaching regarding how to make use of the fact that different students have certain preferences for learning and also strengths for using what they have learned. Most have been very complicated and almost impossible to implement in classrooms, which hold up to thirty students with a myriad of intelligences and learning styles and preferences. Some have suggested that we teach everything in seven different learning centers so that each student can learn in his or her preferred learning modality; now that could get very complex and would require an unbelievable amount of work.

Let's look at some practical uses of the knowledge we have gained through research on the multiple intelligences. Without being too elementary or simplistic, since we know that there are at least these seven "intelligences," learning styles, or learning modalities; all we need to do is regularly incorporate each of the modalities as we teach. This does not mean that each lesson is written in seven different modalities, or taught as students go to centers where their own specific modality is being utilized! The idea of allowing students to learn only in their preferred modality sounds great, but would be impossible to implement. I do not know many teachers who would attempt to write the lesson in seven modalities and then try to moderate each one thus individualizing instruction based on each individual's learning style. In most educational scenarios except for possibly home schooling, instruction is given to fairly large groups. We do not have the luxury of private, one on one teaching, and thus find ourselves teaching to the average and teaching to the learning style we feel is most prominent in our classroom. In order to address the fact that there are at least seven learning modalities in our classrooms, we must try to use each modality if not every day or every other day, at least once a week. Though at first glance we might think it impossible, it is not difficult to use all seven every day and in every class.

Let's use teaching long division of two or more digits as an example, and presume that this is the first day that we introduce this skill to our fourth grade students. We are trying to incorporate the seven intelligences in our teaching modalities for the day: verbal, logical, visual, musical, physical, intrapersonal, and interpersonal. We could use words to say and write the steps on the board. We could then review these steps (estimate, divide, multiply, subtract, compare, bring down; e, ÷, ×, -, c, ↓), to the musical ♫ tune of "Oh my Darling Clementine" (Estimate ♫, Divide ♫, Multiply ♫, and Subtract ♫, Compare ♫, and Bring down ♫, now we do it all again ♫.) Then we could review the steps once more, but this time with everyone standing and shaking their hips between each step, then finally, we could divide into groups of two and have one student explain it to the other, then have the two solve an actual problem using the steps we have taught. And finally, we could let the students work a few problems independently. We have very quickly, but efficiently used every intelligence as we taught two or more digit long division. Not only did we specialize in each of our student's learning modality, we gave every student the opportunity to experience learning through a modality that may not have been his own. Sound like fun? It will be both for you as you use your creativity in looking for ways to allow students to use their learning intelligence, and for our students enabling them to learn in a format that is easiest for them.

Now, we may not be able to use all seven intelligences in every lesson, but we can incorporate all of them throughout a week or a month, or a unit of instruction. We may be teaching a university class, and may use the common mode of lecture to which we can always add the visuals through a power point presentation expressed in a logical outline format. Then we could ask our students to come up with a musical or physical way to remember the facts or ideas. Finally, we could have our students work as a group out of class to come up with an innovative way to implement or demonstrate the use of this knowledge. For those interpersonal learners, we could occasionally have our students self-teach a concept then bring their findings back to the classroom. I hope that you are getting the idea of what I am referring to regarding using the different intelligences as we teach a concept. Since students have their own individual best way to learn, we can also help them to discover what their intelligences might be, and encourage them to translate our presentations into their own modality. For example, we are studying American Literature, and have organized our study by authors and time periods. The visual learner might need to see a sketch of the face of the author and a picture to summarize each of his literary works. The logical learner will probably organize his notes in an outline format by periods, authors and works. The physical learner may put a movement to each author and work, and the intrapersonal learner may get together with a study group to discuss each author and work. The verbal learner may say his or her notes out loud when studying. Just as mapping the authors and titles would not be the best way for some students to study, writing a jingle of the authors and titles or studying in a group would not be the best study mode for other students; but each student should know his own modality and study in the way that best fits his or her learning style or intelligence.

In summary, the many articles which have been written regarding multiple intelligence and learning styles, must be translated into practical classroom instructional methods and practical student study methods. We cannot teach the same lesson seven times each time using a different modality, but we can incorporate all of the different modalities in one lesson or at least in one lesson each week or month or unit. If as educators we are to take full advantage of the wonderful research and findings regarding intelligence, then we must consistently ask ourselves, "What am I doing with this wonderful information which the research has given me?"

PRIMACY-RECENCY EFFECT

Another very interesting finding of brain research is the "Primacy-Recency Effect". Put very simply, the brain, like national television has "prime time" programming and "down time" programming. During prime time, the brain is at its highest level of functioning, thus providing us as educators prime teaching opportunities. Obviously, during "down time", we would do better by not trying to teach new, difficult, or demanding topics. Prime time lasts no more than thirty minutes, and of course varies by age from three minutes for a preschooler to thirty minutes for a mature adult learner. We will usually find the brain's "prime time" at the beginning of a session, therefore we should take full advantage of this time instead of wasting it on taking attendance etc...After utilizing the brain's full prime time capabilities, we will need to give our students a short break maybe adding some movement, stretching, change of scenery, water, or even nutrition so that the down time is well utilized. With the human learner, in addition to "Prime Time 1" (optimal functioning) and "down time" (time the brain requires to file and to organize); there is also a "Prime Time 2". Though "Prime Time 2" is not as efficient as "Prime Time 1", This period of time can be utilized for effective review, for teaching less crucial subtopics, for doing guided practice, etc..., and can last as long as Prime Time One does (two minutes for every year of age up to 30 minutes).

Now this Primacy-Recency concept may seem a little hard to implement, but again to put it as simply as possible, we can best utilize this research finding by consciously creating the learning segments according to the "Prime 1", "Down", and "Prime 2" cycles of our students. Our students will remember best what is presented first in a learning segment (Prime Time One); second best what is presented last (Prime Time Two); and least what is presented right in the middle of our segments (Down Time). For example, if I am teaching high school students whose "Prime Time" may last for thirty minutes (15 years old times two minutes per year), then I would want to use the first thirty minutes of class reviewing previously taught material and introducing the new material of the day. We would not, though this is pretty much practice in most classrooms, want to waste prime time on taking attendance and checking homework. Since most high school classes are fifty minutes long, we could stop and check homework after the first thirty minutes. Incorporating some sort of movement, hydration, nutrition, etc... during this time would set our students up for another fifteen minutes of "Prime Time 2". During these last minutes of class, we could do some "guided practice" (Remember this term from chapter five?) some additional review, a little independent practice and then the final "blessing". Understanding these principles of how the brain functions at its utmost, we should not attempt to present new material, or lecture for more than thirty minutes. We should also allow and plan for the "Down" time, and then again take full advantage of Prime Time 2". If we are teaching younger children, then we must create teaching segments which for a six year old, would include a maximum of twelve minutes of rigorous learning time with considerations for "Down" time and then taking full advantage of the "Prime Time 2". In summary, let's take advantage of PT1 to teach our main points; DT to give a short break, present details or elaborate on items that may not be necessary to hold on to, and PT2 to summarize and review main ideas and concepts.

To conclude this chapter, I would just like to encourage us not to get too concerned by the much technical information that is available. Let's use the important knowledge that the research has given us in practical ways that will help our students learn more easily and at optimal brain functioning levels. True wisdom as we have discussed previously means applying the vast knowledge that we gain understanding of. I know that we will all utilize some of the practical ideas presented here, and add many more to them. Of course, our students will benefit as we incorporate and apply the brain research findings to our teaching methods. In the next month, work on some of the "wisdom" suggestions listed below and note the effects on your students' learning. In the next chapter, we will gain some very practical ideas on how to effectively teach and handle those wonderful and challenging "exceptional students".

APPLICATION (WISDOM)

1. *Write in your lesson plans one of the six key points to work on during the next six weeks of class. Each week, incorporate the knowledge and ask your students to evaluate the effects of each.*

2. *Share the information on oxygen, nutrition, and rest with parents at the next opportunity, or put it in a letter to them. Ask every student to bring a water bottle and two healthy snacks daily.*

3. *In the next month, put two sets of required learning information to a well-known song or ask a musically inclined student to do it for you. Try playing music when you are not actually instructing and note the effects on your students.*

4. *Organize your class periods using the PT1, DT, and PT2 principles.*

5. *Take two to three minutes daily to "Inspire" your students and prepare them emotionally so that they can utilize their brains more effectively.*

6. *Oxygenize your students often by allowing them to move and note the effects.*

Chapter Eight

EVERYTHING YOU NEED TO KNOW ABOUT THE EXCEPTIONAL LEARNER

Key Points

1. *"Exceptional" students are those students who are not like every other student, those that require a different type of attention and a different type of teaching, and those who have to overcome various barriers in order to learn.*

2. *Some of the most common barriers of learning are Attention Disorders in which students are challenged with focusing; Academic Skills Disorders where students are challenged in acquiring the three "R's" of reading, writing and arithmetic; and Developmental Language Disorders in which students are challenged with articulation, expression, and receiving language.*

3. *The Law (Section 504 Rehabilitation Act of 1973) requires that students with diagnosed learning disabilities be provided equal access and opportunities to learn in public educational institutions.*

4. *Effective strategies for working with exceptional students will include the following: proper communication, social support, a routine environment, modified assignments and assessments, varied methods of material presentation.*

5. *There are specific strategies for students with attention deficits, for hyperactive students, and for students with other visual and motor processing delays.*

What we have learned thus far regarding line upon line teaching, teaching with "pizzazz" and practical brain research will help as we tackle this very important topic of the "Exceptional learner". In fact, understanding our role as teachers to influence every student (this includes the exceptional learner) who will in turn influence his or her world, learning to touch the hearts of our students so they can trust us with their minds, and preparing adequately will also assist us greatly as we reach the exceptional learner. And finally, understanding discipline and maintaining good class control will be a positive factor in reaching these learners.

Exceptional students – who are they, how do they learn, how can I truly reach them and make a difference in their lives? When we consider the word "exceptional", we think of a student that is not like every other student; one that is different from the rest, one that is the exception to the rule, one that actually stands out. We have all had these students that require a different type of attention and a different type of teaching. These students have frustrated, challenged, sharpened and even saddened us. We have spent many hours thinking about them, and wondering if we are even capable of reaching them. I would like for this chapter to be one that encourages and inspires us as we learn more about these special students and how they learn so that we can truly reach them! The title of this chapter is "Everything You Need to Know About the Exceptional Learner", and as with all of the other chapters, I will keep it very simple and very practical. We will discuss ways to discover the exceptional students in our classrooms (not difficult as anything exceptional stands out right away); we will discuss not only how they learn, but how they think; and finally we will learn some strategies and methods for actually teaching these special students.

Did you know that approximately 20% of any school population could be considered to be exceptional? Did you also know that about 80% of the populations in prisons were exceptional students frustrated right into lives of crime? Did you know that some of the most brilliant people who have ever lived, such as Albert Einstein, Thomas Edison, Tom Cruise, Walt Disney, Greg Louganis, Beethoven, Mozart, and Da Vinci were exceptional individuals? You might be totally agreeing that they are all very exceptional inventors, entertainers, musicians, athletes, etc., but did you know that though not all were diagnosed, all had many of the symptoms of what today we call learning disabilities? Though school for these people was somewhat of a nightmare, we will all agree that they are very successful people. Fortunately, this possible one per cent of that twenty percent of individuals with learning challenges or differences became successful in spite of their school experiences.

Who or what made the difference in their lives and kept them out of prisons and from the lives that the majority of these individuals experience? Did all of them have mothers like Thomas Edison's who in spite of what his teacher thought, believed that her son had something to offer mankind, removed him from a system which would not build his self-esteem and nurtured his inquisitive and brilliant mind. Read this excerpt from his biography by Gerald Beals:

At age seven – after spending 12 weeks in a noisy one-room schoolhouse with 38 other students of all ages – Tom's overworked and short tempered teacher finally lost his patience with the child's persistent questioning and seemingly self-centered behavior. Noting that Tom's forehead was unusually broad and his head was considerably larger than average, he made no secret of his belief that the hyperactive youngster's brains were "addled" or scrambled.

If modern psychology had existed back then, Tom would have probably been deemed a victim of ADHD (attention deficit hyperactivity disorder) and prescribed a hefty dose of the "miracle drug" Ritalin. Instead, when his beloved mother – whom he recalled *"was the making of me... [because] she was always so true and so sure of me... And always made me feel I had someone to live for and must not disappoint."* – became aware of the situation, she promptly withdrew him from school and began to "home-teach" him. Not surprisingly, she was convinced her son's slightly unusual demeanor and physical appearance were merely outward signs of his remarkable intelligence.

With this chapter, I would like to inspire us to be the teachers who have the vision to see greatness in each one of our students, exceptional or not, to understand them and their learning needs, and to be equipped to teach them.

TERMINOLOGY AND THE STIGMA OF IT

Up to this point, I have used the term exceptional to describe these students with average to above average intelligence whose achievement as measured by our educational system does not match this intelligence. I love the term exceptional because it so accurately describes these students, and so hate the term Learning Disabled because it so communicates disability, inability, impairment, restriction, disqualification to learn; and because it seems so permanent a label. The Webster definition of a learning disability is both accurate and helpful in understanding exceptional students:

Any of various conditions (as dyslexia) that interfere with an individual's ability to learn and so result in impaired functioning in language, reasoning, or academic skills and that are thought to be caused by difficulties in processing and integrating information.

I would also like for us to consider a definition of one disability by Frank Klein who is himself autistic:

Autism itself is not the enemy... the **barriers to development** that are included with autism are the enemy. The **retardation that springs from a lack of development** is the enemy. The **sensory problems that are often themselves the barriers** are the enemy. These things are not part of who the child is... they are barriers to who the child is meant to be, according to the developmental blueprint. Work with the child's strengths to overcome the weaknesses, and work within the autism, not against it, to overcome the developmental barriers. "

I love Klein's statement that these barriers are not who the child is, but barriers to who he is meant to be. The student is not disabled, there are certain "barriers" in his learning that are trying to keep him from being who is meant to be. I strongly believe that if we can get a proper perspective of this point, and acquire some useful knowledge regarding these learning barriers, and learn some effective teaching skills which will not only help our exceptional learners, but all of our students; then we can influence the lives of these students and launch them to greatness instead of forcing them into failure.

I would like to define learning in very, very simple terms. All learning requires for information to come into the brain from the senses (sight, hearing, touch, even smell and taste). The brain must then process (understand and file for future use) this information. Finally, the brain must then recall the information and get it out through speech, writing, or application (doing, such as flying the airplane or driving the car). Exceptional students encounter barriers in one or many parts of this learning model. Sometimes a student cannot focus on what is being taught (attention deficit); sometimes the student's visual perception of what is being taught is scrambled (dyslexia); sometimes a student needs movement in order to focus (hyperactivity); sometimes a student cannot put on paper what he can say with his mouth (motor processing problems); sometimes a student cannot remember what he learned two days ago (long term memory processing problems) and so on and so forth. The list of barriers is long and there are many technical terms used for these barriers or challenges, but I have compiled a quick reference list with some very simplified definitions:

1. Attention Disorders; students are challenged with focusing

   - ADD (Attention Deficit Disorder); Students whose attention is on everything in their environment thus challenged to focus on what is being taught.

   - HD (Hyperactivity Disorder); Students are overly active thus are challenged with controlling brain and physical activity long enough to focus on what is being taught.

   - ADHD (Attention Deficit/with Hyperactivity Disorder); Numbers one and two above together. Inattention and distractibility, restlessness, inability to sit still, and difficulty concentrating on one thing for any period of time.

2. Academic Skills Disorders; students are challenged in acquiring the three "R's" of reading, writing and arithmetic.

   - Dyslexia (Language Skills Disorders); Students who have difficulty recognizing and processing graphic symbols (letters) thus challenged in learning to read and comprehending reading,

   - Writing and Spelling Disorders. Students are challenged with vocabulary, grammar, and memory needed to compose, write, and spell correctly.

   - Arithmetic Disorders; Students are challenged with deciphering symbols, order, sequence, directionality, etc... needed in math.

3. Developmental Language Disorders; Students are challenged with articulating language, expressing language, and decoding or receiving language; therefore cannot communicate their thoughts verbally

While reading this abridged list, we could note that all of us have some sort of learning challenge or barrier. Our exceptional students usually have more than one barrier and at some more severe levels than the average individual. At this point, I would like to share with you my proven philosophy regarding exceptional students and really all students. It is simply: All students can learn! Our exceptional students have normal brains and average to high intelligence and struggle with barriers which block the reception, processing, or application of what is learned. Though I do believe that every individual is blessed with certain gifts and abilities, and that some students have strengths in one area as opposed to another; I am not of the opinion that some individuals just cannot learn certain things; therefore, we should just concentrate on their strengths and forget their weaknesses. This would be fine, if we were just talking about learning to play an instrument as opposed to learning to play a sport, but when it comes to reading and writing and communicating and performing mathematical calculations, I am sorry, but we cannot just ignore these vitally important skills necessary to exist on this planet. Thus, we must remove or even go around the barriers which keep students from this type of learning. For example, I may not have been gifted with musical ability and will never be a Richard Clayderman or Mozart or Kenny G, but I can learn to play the piano or saxophone or any other musical instrument. Though not all of our students will be writers or mathematicians or eloquent speakers, every single one of them can learn to read and to write and to do math and to communicate! It is a matter of breaking down those "barriers" by training their brains to do what is challenging but not impossible! Here, I repeat my philosophy of learning: All students can learn!

IDENTIFYING THE EXCEPTIONAL STUDENT

Though as I mentioned before, our exceptional students are readily identified because they will always stand out as being a little different, or learning a little differently than the average students in our class, I believe that once a student stands out in this way, that we must get some confirmation that we are indeed dealing with a learning challenge and not with some other situation. Over the years, I have found that when there is such a student in our classrooms, teachers are inclined to explain the issue by stating that the student is just "lazy". Because part of the nature of these students is that one day they seem to have it and the next day or week not, many teachers come to this faulty conclusion. Sometimes there are other issues such as home problems, lack of nutrition, etc...that a student is going through which impedes his learning, and sometimes a student truly is challenged by a learning barrier. How can we know the difference? A practical rule of thumb would be that when we and the students' parents have met and exhausted all of our resources of helping to re-enforce instruction both at school and at home with little success, there is a possibility that there is a learning barrier. Note the words "exhausted all." As many parents, I too am opposed to labeling students too quickly and without first making every effort to teach a student. Many times children who have not been taught discipline are too quickly labeled ADHD, or children who have little language skills prior to beginning school are labeled dyslexic, but when we have worked extensively in the classroom and partnered with parents re-enforcing at home and do not get results, then it is time to explore the possibility of a more serious learning barrier or challenge.

When we as educators feel that there might be something more serious than the need for additional re-enforcement from home, we must be very wise in communicating this to parents. I strongly recommend that we as teachers and administrators be very cautious with our language as we suggest to parents the possibility of their child having a more serious learning issue. This is the last thing that a parent wants to hear about their precious child. I have found over the years that if parents have not seen that we as teachers and they as parents have done everything possible first, then they will usually deny that there is any problem. But if they have gone through the effort and sometimes agony of working with their student for hours and hours only to find that they still could not spell those words or remember those facts, then they are more open to our suggestion that there may be something more serious to consider.

It is at this point that we as educators can suggest that we get an educational diagnosis of what may be the problem with their student's learning. At this point, we will need to consult with an educational psychologist who is qualified and trained to administer and interpret an IQ test to insure that there is no form of brain damage and that the student is functioning at average and above intelligence levels. Secondly, we must consult with an educational diagnostician who will measure the student's achievement on various academic tasks. If the intelligence quotient is average or above and the achievement is below average, then we know that the student has a learning barrier, and with the help of our diagnosticians, we can even know what type of barrier the student has.

THE LAW AND EXCEPTIONAL STUDENTS

The Law (Section 504 Rehabilitation Act of 1973) states that "qualified individuals with disabilities in the United States" shall not be excluded from participating in or denied the benefits of, or be subjected to discrimination under any program receiving federal financial assistance. In other words, students with diagnosed learning disabilities must be provided equal access and opportunities to learn in public educational institutions. If a "qualified" student attends a private school, then they are entitled to the services for exceptional students provided by public educational institutions. Of course it is our desire for all students to succeed in school, and we would not desire to deny an exceptional student the right to a good education. The law notes that the students must be "qualified", and this means properly diagnosed as mentioned above. I strongly believe that sometimes we begin to treat students before we have actual proof that they indeed have a learning challenge. Too many students are diagnosed by the words of their parents or by their teachers before we have actual professional opinions from experts in the field. Once we have proof of our assumption that there is a learning barrier, then and only then should we begin to make the accommodations and, or modifications which this act describes. If we make them before we have a diagnosis, then we will probably never convince the parent that there are special needs.

MODIFICATIONS AND ACCOMMODATIONS

Let's define both terms and then discuss their implementation and their effect on the student's learning. An accommodation is an adjustment in methods, quantity of work, testing conditions, seating arrangement, etc...that will enhance a student's ability to learn. It does not affect the type of grade a student will receive, and can range from having a student sit in close range of the teacher, to keeping him on task with a timer, to testing the student orally, to allowing the student to record a lecture in addition to taking notes. We will discuss accommodations in detail in the later part of this chapter, but what is important to note is that an accommodation does not change what is being taught or measured; only how the student is being taught and measured. A modification on the other hand changes the learning objectives for the course or grade level required of the student, and therefore requires a written contract and a notation on the report card or transcript that such alterations have been made. We should be cautious about deciding to make modifications and thus lower the level of what a student learns before exhausting all types of accommodations first. Most students with learning challenges can function well if we will just make some accommodations. Modifications would include those items which would actually affect the grade a student received such as lowering the level of tested material, teaching and testing below the student's grade level, allowing a student to use aids such as a calculator, etc... Sometimes it is hard to determine between an accommodation and a modification, but it is important to do so in order to preserve the integrity of our grading and reporting. It would be deceitful to make modifications and not note this fact on a transcript. It would be just as detrimental to retain an exceptional student in the same grade year after year because the student cannot demonstrate achievement and learning on standardized tests. We must remember here that due to processing problems, exceptional students cannot always demonstrate what they actually know.

I would also like to note here that as early as a student is able to understand, no later than in fifth grade or age ten, we must be very honest with him regarding the barriers that he faces while learning. At the same time, we must also emphasize regularly the fact that he is indeed intelligent and highly gifted in areas that other students may not be. Let's not try to fool ourselves or the student; they are indeed exceptional – not disabled.

UNDERSTANDING THAT EXCEPTIONAL STUDENT

As I write this section, I begin to weep at the thought of the frustration, pain, fear, anxiety, and damage that our lack of understanding and ignorance regarding exceptional students causes them. Contrary to the belief of most, they are not just lazy; they are not stupid; they are not retarded; they are not just pretending. They are intelligent, gifted individuals who know but cannot retrieve what they know; who understand but cannot demonstrate that understanding; who desire to be still and obedient but who cannot stop moving; who want to focus, but cannot. I implore us all as teachers to understand this and act accordingly. Do not discipline them or embarrass them for that which they cannot control. If they could, they would so readily do it, but they cannot, so what do we do with them? First, understand and consider what we have just read – if they could, they would. Allow this understanding to lead you in mercy and love and patience as you teach them. Their exceptionality is not their fault or their intent, but it is their responsibility. Be willing to teach them how to be responsible for and deal with their exceptionality. We will deal with this topic in detail in the next section, but for now the most important thing is to acknowledge and believe that they have some learning and behavioral issues that impede their learning and that may also interfere with the learning of the other students in our classes.

ACADEMIC AND PROCESSING DISORDERS

We have already gathered knowledge on the different learning challenges and issues that our exceptional students have. Now it is important for us as educators to understand them. As we mentioned in the previous paragraph, the fact that these students are unable to finish the same amount of work that others do in the same amount of time does not mean that they are lazy, slow, or incompetent. These students require more time to do their work due to processing delays, blockages, or even entanglements. Understand this and your frustration levels and theirs will lessen. Understand that when you ask them a question, their "wheels" are working very hard to retrieve that answer or to understand the question, therefore give them non-pressured time to respond. This may mean that you let them know you will come back to them, or maybe that you call on them only if they volunteer. Understand that some respond better orally than in written format and allow them this option. Let's also understand that they are trying with all their might to learn the math concept or to read that little paragraph we have assigned, and become fearful and frustrated when they see that they cannot catch the concept as quickly as some of the other students.

HYPERACTIVITY AND ATTENTION DEFICIT DISORDERS

Let's understand those who struggle to focus or to stay still and quiet. They are not daydreaming and do not think you are boring, but are paying attention to everything and everyone while you are expecting them to pay sole attention to you. They are not just plain being disobedient and rebellious; doing their own thing. The fact is that they are paying attention to everything that is around them and cannot seem to screen out the sound of the students playing outside the classroom window, or that clock ticking away at the front of the room, or those two students who are talking behind them. And those who seem to have the wiggles and the woggles who constantly tap and rock and even spin; again, understand that they don't just want to move, they must move! Think of it this way, if we had ants in our pants or had an incredible itch, and someone tried to keep us from rolling on the ground or rubbing against the wall to scratch, how would that feel? This is how the hyperactive student feels when we want to tie him in his chair for two hours straight!

DEVELOPMENTAL LANGUAGE DISORDERS

And finally, let's understand that our students are not trying to be funny or sarcastic when they seem to answer a question we did not ask, or one that we asked a few minutes ago. These students sometimes have difficulty sequencing their thoughts or in general, just communicating them. We also need to understand that these barriers can also cause social problems between them and other students and that these exceptional students are often ostracized, ridiculed, and left out by their classmates because of their sometimes "quirky or untimely responses. As we demonstrate our understanding of these students through tolerance and patience and kindness, our students will learn from us and do the same.

Though it is impossible to explain and seek understanding for every type of learning challenge, a good rule of thumb for all students would be to acknowledge the fact that if a student is not learning or even behaving there is always a reason for this. We should be slow to show our frustration or anger, and quick to seek to understand what is causing the problem. In the next session, we will discuss practical strategies for working with exceptional students; we will take into consideration the fact that we have many students and cannot give all of our attention and time to these students, nor jeopardize lowering the academic standards and goals of the entire group so that our challenged students can keep up.

EFFECTIVE AND PRACTICAL STRATEGIES AND METHODS

This is probably the most important section of this chapter, and I would like to begin by saying that I understand the position of most teachers in respect to these special students. First of all, we have a responsibility to insure that the majority reach their potential and the objectives which have been given to us to teach. Secondly, most teachers receive too little training regarding exceptional students, and therefore do not know what to do with them. I sincerely believe that we have obtained some valuable knowledge and understanding in the previous paragraphs of this chapter. Now we must demonstrate our wisdom by taking action steps which will really help our students. I also want to state here that if the challenges or barriers are mild, these methods will help to remove the barriers altogether. For those students who have very severe barriers, additional one on one intervention by parents and other professionals such as speech pathologists or educational therapists will be necessary. One thing is for certain, the use of these strategies and methods will definitely keep us from damaging these students emotionally and educationally, so let's begin with some strategies that will benefit students with different barriers. Then we will offer some methods and strategies for the three specific categories which we mentioned when we defined learning disabilities.

STRATEGIES WHICH WILL INSURE EMOTIONAL AND MENTAL CONFIDENCE AND ESTEEM

We have discussed this throughout this book, but it is worth mentioning again and again. All students need to feel welcomed, loved, and understood if they are to succeed. Positive words along with demonstrated concern are probably the most important strategies which we could use to help build the emotional confidence, mental security, and positive self-esteem so needed by these students. Another very important factor is the quick diagnosis of the learning barrier so that accommodations are made before a student begins to feel frustrated, exasperated and defeated. If we did only these two things, it would make such a great amount of difference in the academic and even social lives of these exceptional students!

COMMUNICATION WITH EXCEPTIONAL STUDENTS

Concrete and specific communication helps all students, but is especially helpful for our exceptional students. We should avoid vague vocabulary, instructions and questions such as "later", "maybe", "why did you do that", or "whatever you want to write about will be alright". Also, avoid idioms, double meanings and sarcasm as these students are very literal. Slowing down the pace of instruction or communication in general helps the slow processor, and specifically getting their attention visually, verbally, or physically is very effective. Always break large tasks down into smaller ones. When possible, communicate with all of the modalities (verbal, written, action, demonstration).

Since these students rarely advocate for themselves, we want to encourage communication with them by pausing, listening and waiting for their responses. Watch and listen for their attempts to respond, and give them a positive response such as "great thinking" even when their response is incorrect. Without correcting them, give them the correct answer. Students with obstinate compulsive disorders should be given a choice so that they feel in control even though you provide the choices. Finally, encourage them to communicate thus showing them that their opinions and answers are important.

SUPPORT EXCEPTIONAL STUDENTS SOCIALLY

Because the need to feel socially accepted has such a strong influence on whether a student learns and actually allows himself to be taught, it is very important that we provide our exceptional students with some support in this area. Of course and once again, we set the stage for the degree of acceptance our students will offer to these students by demonstrating our own acceptance of them to our students. We can encourage social interaction by protecting the student from bullying or teasing and praising his classmates when they treat him with compassion and understanding. We can create learning situations where the exceptional student can demonstrate his proficiencies or gifting, and group him with students with common interests and strengths. "Buddies" give the student an advocate, as well as providing academic support. We can practice social skills by setting up situations with one peer, then adding additional peers. We can even teach our exceptional students social skills by modeling, and rehearsing with them skills such as taking turns, complimenting others, greeting, repairing breakdowns, accepting the success of others, and even joking and teasing. We can concentrate on changing unacceptable and odd behaviors by demonstrating, discussing, and practicing more appropriate ones.

PROVIDE A ROUTINE ENVIRONMENT

Change is sometimes difficult for exceptional students to adjust to readily; therefore, we should strive for a predictable and orderly environment, minimizing transitions. Exceptional students will thrive in classrooms that have a lot of order and tight discipline. We should avoid surprises, talk the student through stressful situations, and always prepare him for special activities, altered schedules and other changes. Finally, we will want to avoid sensory overloads and distractions by locating the student in a low stimulus spot in the classroom.

PRESENTATION OF MATERIAL

Use as many types of presentation methods as possible; visual, verbal, written, pictured, objects, demonstrations, maps/charts/diagrams, computer, music, motion, and video. When possible and without becoming boring, use established routines (inspire, review, introduce new material, practice, review, bless). Divide the teaching into small and sequential steps. Review and allow many opportunities to practice. Give the student prompts and clues to help him remember or get started. Insure the support of parents for further practice and review by providing them with review sheets of the essentials of what is being taught. Check understanding frequently by having the student repeat instructions, material, or assignments.

Alert the student to important points by saying, "This is important", or "Listen carefully", or "Write this down". Connect new material with previously learned material by demonstrating how they relate. Keep the rate of presentation at an average pace.

ASSIGNMENTS AND ASSESSMENTS

We can always shorten assignments and tests as long as every type of problem is practiced or tested; increase the amount once the student is able to do what is assigned in the same amount of time as other students. A good rule for homework is one hour through third grade, and two hours from fourth through high school excluding special projects. Use multiple choice questions when possible rather than fill in the blank. Extra time after school or during lunch to complete a test can be allowed. Show the student how learning applies to real situations. Teach the student to manage himself through a timer, contracts, and visual cues from you. Students must be given reinforcement individually, immediately, and concretely. Students should be able to use strengths daily.

To help students stay on task, break assignments down into smaller units and check between each unit in order to give him frequent feedback and redirection. Let the student sit next to his buddy who can assist, remind to return to task or to listen, and insure that assignments are copied correctly and completely. Show him how to use a checklist, prioritize tasks, and complete them according to time available and priority of tasks.

Specific strategies for students with ADD

1. Physically touch them often to bring them back into focus.

2. Remove unnecessary stimulus that competes with instruction (visual, audio, smell, other senses)

3. Say their name as you teach to refocus them.

4. Place a timer that actually ticks on their desk to draw attention to the task at hand.

5. Mask a test or assignment allowing the student to see only one problem or question at a time; thus avoiding the frustration attempting a large task.

Strategies specifically for hyperactive students

1. Teach the student to tap their leg with their fingertips in place of making distracting noises by tapping other items.

2. Give him the opportunity to move by providing movement for the entire class during instruction, or just for him by agreement or by wave of a movement pass.

3. Allow hyperactive students to have a chair that rocks or spins safely.

4. Sooth him with the stroke of your hand and quiet voice.

5. Soothe with soft music at very low volume

Dyslexia and other visual and motor processing delays or deficits

1. Students will need much repetition to open brain paths; get parents to do much of this at home. Provide them with the necessary materials and training to do so.

2. Utilize music to learn by and with

3. Let parents read the majority of the reading assignments to the student and have the student read very short selections to avoid frustration.

4. Covering reading materials with colored clear plastic sheets helps some students.

5. Highlight material to be learned or read.

6. Keep extraneous distracters off of material to be read.

7. Be sure that worksheets are clear, simple, and well defined.

8. Avoid having student depend on work copied from the board; provide him with a written copy of your manual or lecture notes.

9. Avoid large amounts of written work (both in class and as homework).

10. Cursive will be an easier form of writing as the student does not pick up his pencil as often.

11. Have acceptable standards for neatness that may not be as high as for the norm.

12. Avoid testing speed and accuracy; test content and mastery instead.

Once again, we could never be all inclusive regarding strategies and methods for the myriad of learning barriers and challenges that exist, but we have discussed enough to get us on our way to effectively meeting the needs of our exceptional students so that they can truly learn. Though I do not expect us to be experts in this field after reading this chapter, I do know that we all have more knowledge and understanding than the typical teacher education graduate, and I encourage you to refer back to this chapter as you encounter and are challenged and inspired by these special students. I will end this chapter with a valuable statement: it is much easier to train a child than to repair an adult. Therefore, let's reach these exceptional students and by doing so, let's believe that our influence in their lives will be such that we will empower them and inspire them to be all that they were destined to be!

APPLICATION (WISDOM)

1. *Make a list of the students you currently have who fit the profile of students with learning challenges. Next to each name, list the characteristics or barriers that keep them from learning. Next to these characteristics, put the name of or the category of the disability or disabilities which describe them.*

2. *Investigate their records or discuss with their parents whether they have noticed some of these learning challenges.*

3. *Return to the text to review the key ways to help them learn, then write out a prescription for each student describing how you will best meet their learning needs.*

4. *Schedule monthly meetings with the parents of these students to set and review plans to help them succeed in your class.*

5. *Meet with your school counselor or administrator to discuss these students and how your school can help meet their learning needs.*

Chapter Nine

SUPERVISION – GUARDING AND PROTECTING OUR STUDENTS AND OUR SCHOOLS

Key Points

1. We guard and protect our students spiritually by preserving their image of who they are.

2. We can protect the mind or the thinking of our students, the will or the desire to do of our students, and the emotions or feelings of our students.

3. We guard and protect the physical well-being of our students through supervision.

4. Effective supervision requires the presence and undivided attention of supervisors, an audible means of communicating or getting the attention of students, and a practiced plan of action in case of emergency.

5. *As we carefully and conscientiously guard and protect our students, we will of course be guarding and protecting our schools from legal liability.*

Thus far in our journey to become great teachers we have learned some important key concepts; we learned that teaching is all about transforming our world through our influence on students – this is why we teach. We learned that before we can teach our students, we must touch their hearts – as we do, our students allow us to teach them. We learned that we must prepare in order to effectively teach our students – therefore, we prepare annually, weekly, and daily. We have learned that we cannot teach our students unless we can manage their behavior and that authority has much to do with discipline. We have learned that we must eat an elephant one bite at a time – thus we lay line upon line as we teach. We have learned that we cannot teach a sleeping anything – thus we teach with "pizzazz". We have learned how to implement the key findings of brain research – thus we take advantage of how the magnificent brain works as we teach. And finally, in the last chapter, we learned about the characteristics of the exceptional students in our classrooms – thus we teach so that all can learn. In this chapter, we will discuss how to guard and protect our students and thus our schools.

Because we have such a strong desire and commitment to teaching and training individuals who will impact and change their worlds, the topic of guarding and protecting both our precious students and our schools is a very important one. To lose even one student or effective school due to ignorance or carelessness could mean the loss of the next great Pulitzer Prize winner, or great leader of a country, or eternity impacting evangelist or pastor, or any other individual whose destiny is to significantly impact the world that we live in. As educators, it is not only our responsibility to teach and train our students, but to guard and protect the lives of those students which are entrusted to us, and the schools in which this training takes place. Our diligence and wisdom in the area of guarding and protecting will insure not only the continuance of the lives of destiny, but of the great schools which have been established to train them. Neglect due to ignorance in this area at worst could result in the loss of the lives and future destiny of our students in addition to legal action against our schools, which could put us out of business. Though we are not supreme beings with the ability to protect from evil, we are indeed intelligent beings who can obtain knowledge and understanding so that we can apply it and thus prevent evil from occurring. This all may sound like a little much, but I sincerely charge every one of us with this serious responsibility of watching out for the security and safety of our students and thus our schools.

Every student is someone's most prized possession, which has been entrusted with much faith into our hands for a large part of their waking hours. We must accept the responsibility of guarding and protecting their entire beings; spirit, soul (mind, will, and emotions), and body. This means guarding what enters their spiritual beings – that this be truth and edifying; guarding what their minds, wills, and emotions are exposed to; and finally, protecting their physical bodies from any harm. At this point, you might think that I am asking us to be teacher, parent, and even body guard; a formidable task without a lot of knowledge, understanding, and wisdom (the application of that knowledge and understanding). In this chapter we will discover some very practical and vital keys regarding this serious task of guarding our students, and though even with these keys we will not be able to prevent every problem; our mere awareness of this teacher responsibility will do much in the way of successfully guarding and protecting our students and thus our schools.

First, we protect and guard our students because we understand that we have been privileged with the task of teaching, training and guiding them. As I mentioned before, they are the most prized and valuable possessions of their parents and even their grandparents. Consider the magnitude of trust which these people have placed in us and in our schools as they send them to us for approximately eight of their fifteen waking hours, five days a week, and nine months a year for approximately seventeen years! We in turn must take on this responsibility with this thought in mind as we diligently endeavor to guard and protect our students from any harm. Our goal should be that our students are always edified, taught and protected spiritually, soulishly (mind, will and emotions) and physically. When we accomplish this, we will have truly guarded and protected them. Now, let us look at each of these areas separately and learn how we can practically guard, protect, and teach them.

GUARDING AND PROTECTING OUR STUDENTS SPIRITUALLY

We will define "spiritual guarding and protecting" as the preservation of our student's inner or true self. This is who they really are; individuals who have been created for a purpose who have within them everything that they will need to accomplish this purpose. As teachers, we must guard what we allow to go into that inner self so that our students are always being encouraged and edified by us as their teachers, by our colleagues and co-laborers, and even by their peers. During the nineties, we experienced the many tragedies of individuals who lashed out at their peers and teachers and even parents after having received their "full" of what I believe is an equal atrocity with physical abuse. I believe that students who were destined to be warriors against evil turned that strength and courage against a system and individuals who were ignorant of the damage they were doing or allowing others to do against them. I do not say this to justify the horrendous actions of the students at Columbine and other places where terror reigned as individuals poured out their anger in a generalized way against their classmates and teachers, but to point out the potential for danger that can exist when those who are in authority (parents, teachers, etc..) do not guard carefully the spirits, souls, and physical bodies of those entrusted to us. Realizing that we are not God or even our students' parents and that we are not omnipresent or omnipotent, we must acknowledge our role in protecting and guarding that very important inner self of our students.

How do we do this? We begin by first understanding that the qualities and character traits of each one of our students are necessary for them to fulfill their destinies. For example, instead of noting their strength and courage as an act of rebellion and anarchy against us as their teachers, we must understand that what they will do in life will require these qualities. We can understand that the student who is so concerned with making sure that every letter written is perfect was made with this incredible need for exactness and precision because of what he will ultimately contribute to society. And that student who loves to be at the center of all activity might just be the next Oscar winner or political leader. And what about that student who sacrifices his work to comfort or help someone who is in need around him? Could he be the next Mother Teresa? Knowing and understanding this principle will help us to see the persons whom our students are destined to become. We can then begin to commend them for these traits and qualities which are natural to them, and to encourage them with the fact that these qualities are very important for them to become what they are destined to become, and finally to channel and direct their behaviors in such a way as to encourage them as we teach them to use these qualities in a very positive way.

Here is an example. Those students who love to talk and hear about what is going on with their classmates' lives are counselors or even pastors in the making. Commend them for their sincere concern for others and help them to keep a confidence and learn good wisdom from which to advise their peers. And those students who constantly come to the defense of others even when the matter does not personally affect them; these are the possible lawyers and judges and even public servants who need to be acknowledged for their concern for others, and then trained in the how and when of defense. There are many examples, but the point here is that in order to guard and protect our students' inner self or spirit, we must study their qualities or bents, understand that they are necessary for them to fulfill their destinies, commend and encourage them for these traits, and finally, show them how these traits or qualities can be used in a positive way.

With our understanding and the words which acknowledge this understanding, we help others such as our co-laborers and our students' peers to understand and appreciate them as we do. Though we cannot control what others do, we can certainly teach and train and correct those who have influence on our students (parents, peers, other teachers). Our students replay what we do and not what we say they should do. Our positive words are a very powerful model for our students and co-laborers.

In addition to being a good example with our own attitudes and our words which demonstrate them, we can also teach our students the important skill of receiving the good from others and sifting out the negative that others sometimes try to put into our lives; the skill of understanding the ignorance of some who speak negatively, and the skill of rejecting that negative input. Our students will then be able to forgive the ignorance and even the hurt which motivates some people to attack or demean them, and guard their inner self so that what others say or think does not affect them. Because of this knowledge and understanding, our students can now choose to discard negatives and even respond with positives. What potential for good we have if in the one quarter, semester or year that we have with our students we could teach them this vital principle! Though it might seem blasphemous in educational circles, I dare to say that this might be as or more important than teaching our academic subjects. Someone once said that many of the most important things that we teach are caught and not taught.

This very important principle is worth summarizing. Guarding and protecting the inner self or the true person or spirit of our students is crucial. We do this by first studying and discovering those particular traits or qualities or characteristics which each of our students was born with. We then begin to encourage them and show them the value of these particular qualities for their future endeavors. Then we train them to use these qualities in a positive way. Our example then influences others who might have influence over our students. When we see or hear others speaking negatively, we help them to understand the power of their influence and endeavor to help them see and speak positively. Finally, since we cannot control others, we train our students in the important skill of understanding where the negatives come from, filtering them out, and receiving the positive.

GUARDING AND PROTECTING SOULISHLY (MIND, WILL, EMOTIONS)

When we take care of guarding the Spirit (inner person, true person) of our students, we take the first step to protecting the soulish part of our students, because as our students believe in their heart or inner self, this is how they will be. We must move from believing we are or can to actually being or doing what we believe. Therefore, our next responsibility will be to guard and protect the soul – the mind, the will, and the emotions. With the mind, we think, with the will we decide and do, and with the emotions we feel. All three are very important in determining our course in life. We can believe that we can accomplish something, but if we have no will to do it, or if our emotions keep us from doing it then we are still stopped. Therefore, as we guard the spirits of our students by protecting them from negatives, we must also protect the mind or the thinking of our students, the will or the desire to do of our students, and the emotions or feelings of our students. This may seem like a difficult task as the elements of the soul seem to be so inside of our students, but we can actually influence this part of our students.

Since the mind is where they think, we can help our students to think on things that are good. Even though there is a lot of bad in the world, we can help our students to think about is that there is always hope and a solution to the bad. Even though Math or statistics might be difficult for our students, the good thing to think about is that they will have our help in getting through it, and they will indeed get through it. I remember taking a statistics course for my doctoral work in a two week summer module. We all thought we would die and probably flunk with so much difficult material coming our way so quickly, and with so much homework that was so difficult to do. Nevertheless, thanks to a great inspiring teacher (Dr. Marilou Miller, Oral Roberts University), we made it through the course, learned a lot, and I even managed to get an "A". Of course we had to have help dealing with the conflicts between what our minds thought and what our professor was telling us.

Using this same example, it was necessary for our professor to guard and protect our will. Our will is where we decide and then do. I believe that all human beings are born with strong wills which will enable us to face the challenges that life brings us. I also believe that a person's will can get worn down if we do not handle the challenges of life in a positive way. A good lesson to teach and live by is that every challenge, victory or defeat is an opportunity to grow from. Even though our student failed the last history test, or has failed many a spelling test, or even their comprehensive exams, each failure tells us where we need to grow, and if we can instill in our students this principle, then they will (decide and do) it better and better. Notice the pun on words, they will (decide and do) better and better. Have you heard the insane teaching that we must break a child's will by the age of two; or the other insane one that we must not correct or spank a child in fear of breaking their will? Either trying to break their will or purposing not to challenge them so it will not be broken is counterproductive. The first will make their will stronger and the last will make it weaker based on no challenges. I believe that it is human nature to fight back with that will that we are born with. I do not deny that sometimes people (students are people too) do lose the desire to continue, but it takes a lot for a person to get to this point. If our students have lost their desire to keep trying, I would ask us to consider why, and begin to encourage (give them new courage) to try again (do again). We have helped our students believe in their hearts that they can do great things. Their minds are convinced that they can, and they have willed (decided to do) to do so. We have helped to guard their inner self and their soul, and we are set! Wrong!

We have one last aspect of the soul to deal with – the emotions. The emotions are what we feel with; joy, anger, zeal, sadness, apathy, etc... Many times, either challenges or our own or other people's responses to how we have faced the challenges can affect our emotions. Our emotions can paralyze us and keep us from moving forward or they can propel and launch us forward. How can we guard and protect the emotions of our students? We can do so by responding positively to their attempts at meeting challenges. Instead of allowing our students the emotions of defeat, sadness, and then apathy, we must encourage the emotions of challenge, zeal, joy and victory. How do we teach these things? It is not as easy as teaching long division? We walk our students through the challenges; we acknowledge the emotions they are feeling (sadness, fear, defeat, despair); and then we encourage them with other emotions (perseverance, patience, diligence, joy, elation). In this way, we will succeed at guarding and protecting their emotions that all of us were born with; the feelings that will cause us to be victorious and not defeated!

GUARDING AND PROTECTING PHYSICALLY

Now we will discuss what most of us were expecting to hear most about in this chapter. I want to emphasize once more that protecting our students spiritually (in their inner self or true self) and soulishly (in their minds, wills, and emotions) are as important as protecting them physically.

Now that we have re-stated this, we can discuss guarding and protecting the physical well-being of our students. I strongly believe that supervision is the key to this protection. To supervise means to watch over and to be in charge of. Webster's dictionary defines supervision as a critical watching. We must literally, "watch" over. We, or another responsible adult, must be able to actually see our students at all times if we want to properly supervise them. Again, we might argue, I am not God (omnipresent, omnipotent, and omniscient), how can I possibly see them at all times, what about when they are in the restroom or on the playground? Yes, either we or our designated person must literally be able to see our students in order to guard and protect them effectively. This is the most important key to physically guarding and protecting our students; they must be within the sight of the person assigned to watch over them. Obviously, the older our students are, the less we must watch and guard over them because they are able to better guard over themselves, but the following suggestions will definitely apply from cradle to high school and even to college students. I believe that when students are out of sight they are also out of mind, and that the converse of this is also true; if we can literally see them, then we can successfully watch out for their safety.

Let's discuss how we can possibly see our students at all times. First, there should be no hidden corners in our classrooms; when we design learning centers such as a reading center with plush chairs and a nice book case to hold some exciting material, we must position the center in such a way that we can see those working in the center. When students are working in small groups, each group must stay within sight; they cannot go out into the hall to work. When students are at lunch and on the playgrounds, or "social" grounds for high school students, they must stay within the sight lines of those responsible to supervise them; therefore, "blind spots" in these areas must be off limits. In one school where I worked, the play area was shaped in an "L"; students loved to go into the blind spot to play soccer as the play structure took up the majority of the space. Even when positioning myself in the middle of the length of the playground, I could not see both the children playing on the structure and those playing soccer. Therefore, the soccer area was off limits; either all of the children played soccer, or they all played on the structure. The physical location of our students must lie within our line of vision.

Secondly, we must have an "in sight" consciousness as teachers and guardians. No matter what we are doing, we must have wide vision to see what is going on in every part of our supervisory area, and must design our classroom setting accordingly. We have to remind ourselves not to become so focused on the smaller group that we are working with that we forget the entire group. When I am working with a reading circle group in first grade, my circle should be positioned such that I can see the rest of the class, and I must train myself to constantly attend to the rest even though I am focused on the eight students in my circle. This means that when my high school class is working in small groups, each group must work inside the classroom where I can see them. What about restroom breaks, how can I literally watch them, especially when I do not even have a teacher aid? The best solution here is to take group restroom breaks. We stand between the girl's and boy's bathroom listening and watching (guarding and protecting our students). Though we want to protect the privacy of our students, they must know that we have no problem entering if we hear any irregularities. We

can assign students to be our eyes in the restroom and advise us of any problems. What about those times when a student needs to go to the restroom or elsewhere and the whole class cannot go? We want to train them to go when the class goes, but in case of emergencies, always send two. Going to the restroom, send two (one waits outside while the other does his business); going to the office, send two; going to the library or vending machines, send two. We use this "safety in numbers" rule and always send two (mind you, not best friends with best friends, but always looking for a reliable leader to accompany another). Since we all have a tendency to get very engrossed in our teaching, it is wise to set a timer when students leave the classroom to remind us that they have not returned in the three to five minutes allotted to them. Electronic hall passes exist that tell both the student who is out of the classroom and the teacher who is in the classroom that it is time for them to return.

For older students who have breaks between classes, it is vitally important for the teaching staff (who else) to leave the classroom with the students and position ourselves in the hallway right outside of the classroom door (we can watch the classroom and the hall from this vantage point. Those teachers who do not teach in the next period should position themselves in or outside the restroom doors. Our number one supervision rule is that "Students should be visible at all times!" How many restroom fights, drug deals, acts of vandalism etc... could be avoided if this principle was established in every school, both public and private. Many teachers fear the halls and restrooms, yet we send our students there without any supervision! And how about those students who run into the classroom as the tardy bell rings and immediately ask to go to the restroom, their locker, or somewhere else? A rule that will help us guard them properly is that they will be allowed to leave the classroom only for emergencies (forgetting their book in their locker is not an emergency). This may not get us 100% visual accountability, but the higher the percentage of adult supervision and visibility, the better our rate of protection of our students.

The mere presence of an adult is such an effective tool to guard our students against accidents, attacks, or just the foolishness that goes on when more than one young person gets together with another. When older students, or any student or person for that matter, knows that there is someone watching, it is just human nature to do their best. Even adults drive the speed limit when they know that a police officer is positioned up ahead on the freeway. For this same reason, our presence and watchful eye helps our students to be on their best behavior also. We might be thinking, what about teaching our students to do right whether someone is watching or not. This is a very valid point, and it should be our ultimate goal that our students behave appropriately whether someone is watching or not. This goal will certainly be reached as our students develop the habit of doing what is right. It is just like us on the freeway. If we know that our police officers are constantly there, eventually we decide to give up trying to evade the law, and just resolve to drive the speed limit. Our presence and watchful eye will train our students in behavior that is proper when they are at school and with large groups of people.

Let's use lunchroom behavior as an example. Without any teachers or other staff to supervise the students in the cafeteria, our students would just use the same behavior that is acceptable in their homes with families of four to six, but this may not work so well in a lunch room with two hundred persons. Our supervision and watchful eye would teach them that it is not possible to speak as loud as they desire, or to get up whenever they want. We would need to teach them the orderly behavior necessary when such a large group of individuals are together in any place. And then our presence and occasional reminders will help them to actually form great habits. We might be thinking right about this time that we signed up to teach, not to be babysitters and here, I must say that if we do not fulfill this important task of supervision, who will? We might be thinking, "Let the school hire people or get volunteers to do it." This might be a viable option, but it will never be success-ful unless we who are in authority over the students will first instruct and train and require the necessary standard of our students. As a principal, one of the most common petitions of my teachers was to be relieved of lunchroom duty so that they could have a nice quiet lunch break. My response was that I would be happy to allow a volunteer to help with supervision, but only after their class had been instructed and trained in the proper lunch room behavior.

EFFECTIVE SUPERVISION

I believe that effective supervision will require some essential components: presence of sufficient and well trained supervisors based upon the size and complexity of the area and on the number of students being supervised; the undivided attention of those who are supervising; an effective means of getting the attention of those who are being supervised; and a well-known plan of action in cases of emergency. Let's look at each one of these key components separately.

THE PRESENCE OF SUFFICIENT NUMBERS OF TRAINED SUPERVISORS

I would like to note here that it is not difficult to supervise thirty students when they are contained in the classroom and must get permission to move around or even interact with other students. It is much more difficult to supervise students when they are in open areas; therefore the ratios of student to adult supervision must be smaller not larger! While one teacher is completely capable of supervising thirty students contained in a classroom, the task becomes much more difficult when these same thirty students move into a non-contained and larger area. Though the students seem to be occupying themselves with activity, interaction, and conversation; the larger the number of students and the larger the area they are in, the greater the need for supervisors and for attention to what is happening.

Volunteers to assist during these times are highly beneficial. Notice that I said "assist" as we must always have sufficient trained and legally responsible personnel on duty also. Should an emergency arise or an accident occur, parents are usually not going to be satisfied that a parent or student volunteer was the only person on duty at the time; they would expect for an official school person to be on duty also. Most volunteers would not normally be trained in supervising large groups of individuals; therefore, they must receive training in supervision, first aid, and procedures in case of emergencies, and can be especially helpful as we supervise students in larger places such as on the playground.

It is important to mention here that in cases when there is only one person available to supervise students and some are finished with lunch or certain work and want to be outside while the rest of the group is not; since we cannot be in two places at once, the whole group must wait until everyone is finished to go outside. In addition, if we are the only person on the playground, then all students must stay within our visual reach, and if this means that we all play basketball at the courts or we all play on the swings, then so be it.

In many schools, outdoor areas are supervised by coaches and sometimes by volunteers. As I mentioned before, one of the most frequent requests from teachers is that they not have to supervise their students at lunch, recesses, and before and after school. Unfortunately, these are the times when there are the most students in spaces that are much more difficult to supervise. We must insure that our students be supervised by plenty of trained, responsible, and qualified staff people who know what is expected and what to do in emergency situations. They may of course be assisted by volunteers, but we cannot risk the safety and well-being of our students to grant this request of relieving teachers from these duties. And since teachers are so needed during these times, then their preparation and break times must be scheduled throughout the day when students are divided into smaller groups.

PRESENCE AND UNDIVIDED ATTENTION OF SUPERVISORS

Now that we have discussed at length the need for sufficient, qualified, and well trained supervisors of students, we will spend some time discussing how we supervise effectively. The very key point here is that our presence and our attention are both required. Many times we have a "body" on duty, but not the mind; presence, but not attention. We have a teacher supervising a general area, but that person's mind is on the papers that he or she brought out to duty with them to grade, or on the two or three students or one parent who they are holding a conference with while on duty. When we are supervising large groups of students in large and open spaces, we must truly be attending to them, and focusing on what is happening. It takes only a few seconds for an accident or altercation to occur. Therefore the second key to effective supervision is that we must be attending constantly to what is happening; eyes and bodies roving over the area we are supervising to insure that the behavior of our students is safe. Again, we realize that we are not omniscient, omnipotent, or omnipresent, but we truly must make every effort to know what is happening in the entire area that we are supervising. Though it is a lot of fun and also very important to interact with and establish relationship with our students and their parents, our supervisory time is not a good time to work on this. We cannot supervise our students' activity if we are playing basketball with them; we cannot supervise effectively while holding a parent conference on the playground. The precious lives of our students must be our priority when we are called upon to supervise.

In addition to our complete attention while supervising students, it is obvious that we must also be there. The lack of supervision and potential danger to our students because we forgot that it was our duty period or because we allowed ourselves to be detained by a parent or another student leaves our students improperly or inadequately supervised and our schools liable for negligence. When we are scheduled, we must be there, and be there before the students arrive that we are responsible for supervising. This means that we take our own students out with us at least five minutes before our duty begins, and if we have before school duty, we must get to school in time to park, drop our things off, check our mail boxes, and be at our duty post five minutes before the first student is allowed to be on the playground or duty area.

When it is time to leave our posts of supervision, we must be sure that the next person is there to take over, or if we are the last supervisor over this area or these students, we must make sure that any students still on the premises are taken care of. If we are the last persons on the school property, and there are still students who have not been picked up, we must stay with them until someone arrives. This is when cell phones are so handy. I can remember returning from an out of town athletic competition at midnight physically and emotionally tired and ready to go home and get some rest when one student's parents had not arrived to pick them up. It was very tempting to just leave that student there; after all, the parents were advised of what time we would be arriving! Not possible, even though this is a high school student, someone (actually two someone's) must remain with him until his parents arrive! This is part of our responsibility of guarding and protecting our students' safety and our schools' from legal liability. Even though we might reason that these are high school students and even their parents allow them out at night without supervision, and would not sue themselves if something happened to their son who is out alone after midnight, not the case with us. Of course this same procedure would obviously apply if it was 4:00, and our duty was over and a child had not yet been picked up from school. The office is closed and there is no after school service. Both we and the other person on duty with us must stay with the student until their parents arrive. This is not something we would desire to do, but it is something that we must do! The presence of an adult supervisor is required even when there is only one student left!

AUDIBLE MEANS OF COMMUNICATING OR GETTING THE ATTENTION OF THE STUDENTS

In addition to our constant attention to what is happening we should always have a quick and easily audible means of communicating with the students we are supervising. Sometimes our voices may not be loud enough. A whistle, bull horn, or even loud speaker is necessary, and our students must be trained to stop, look and listen when they hear it. This is why it is important for every staff person at a particular school to use the same tool. When we are supervising in a contained classroom, our voice is sufficient, but when supervising larger more open areas with more students, we will need an additional means of getting our students' attention quickly. A key ring that also has a whistle and first aid kit (with band aids, gloves, and mouth protector) can truly be a "life-saver" for both the supervisor and the students he is supervising. Our students must be trained to stop, look to where the sound is coming from, and then listen for instructions when they hear the sound. I have seen many a frustrated first grade teacher try to get all of her students back in line after a recess period with the use of only her voice as well as a high school teacher try to announce the end of the lunch period using only his voice, when we could train our students to get in line or proceed to enter the building with one blow of a whistle. Two blows could mean danger, and the need to listen for instructions, etc... Just as students are trained to respond to the fire, or tornado, or intruder bells, training them to respond to our attention getter device will also insure their safety.

WELL KNOWN PLAN OF ACTION IN CASE OF EMERGENCY

In order to properly guard the physical well-being of our students, we must also have a simple and effective plan of action when emergencies occur. We train and even practice the fire or earthquake or school intruder plans each month or quarter; we should also have a plan and practice that plan for other emergencies. For example, what if we are in the classroom and a student accidentally cuts the tip of his finger off (I have seen this happen both with a first grader and with a high school student)? Or what if we are on the playground with our class and one student falls off the jungle gym and is bleeding profusely (seen this happen many times also)? Do we leave the 99 to help the one? What would you say, take care of the one who might have life threatening injuries or stay and supervise the other students? My response would be that we send two students for help, gather the rest of the students in a place where we can see them and communicate with them, and administer first aid to the student in danger (remember that little first aid kit attached to your key ring and whistle? And by the way, all personnel working in a school from maintenance to cafeteria to office to faculty should be trained in First Aid and CPR as recommended by the Red Cross; this is another effective way of guarding and protecting our students physically). If there was a situation where I, the teacher, was ill or had to leave the classroom, I would ask my partner teacher from across the hall to supervise both her and my group from the hall until I could return. The key is never to leave the larger group of students unsupervised. This would be the procedure if we were alone with our group, but as we have discussed already, when we are supervising larger groups of students in larger areas, we must have sufficient numbers of supervisors so that if an emergency occurred and one supervisor needed to leave the area, there would still be enough supervision to cover the area and the students.

My suggestion for the plan of course is only my suggestion. The key here is that you have a plan that you believe is effective, and that you and your students practice that plan so that when an emergency occurs, they are well trained in what to do. Just like with fire drills and other major emergency drills, sometimes the older students resist and do not take the drills seriously, but they will be thankful that you required them if an emergency ever does occur. I will take a little side track here to say that when we are practicing fire and other emergency evacuation procedures, it is essential that we require our older students to take them seriously and to follow the procedures while drilling these procedures. The fact that we required complete silence during the drill will certainly pay off in case of a true emergency when their life depends on them hearing our instructions.

Another side-track; sometimes teachers and other staff do not take their first aid and CPR training seriously, and even begrudge the time invested in these classes which are required every two or three years; especially when we feel that we never even use what we learn. Proper supervision will help us to avoid using our first aid and CPR skills, but should we ever have to use them, if we have taken them seriously, we will have been so well trained that we will automatically move into action without even thinking, and thus possibly save the life of one of our students.

Another side-track; when accidents occur, a detailed accident report should be completed just as soon as the emergency has been taken care of so that all of the details are still in our memories. This report not only protects the school from liability, but it is also a wonderful tool in order for us to prevent future accidents of the same nature. If there was faulty equipment or inappropriate equipment, we can be sure to rectify this situation and thus prevent another student from exposure to the same danger. It only took one high school student to accidentally slice off the tip of her finger while using the paper cutter and an accident report reviewed by the principal and safety administrator to insure that this piece of equipment was off limits to students. After the accident report of a first grader who "borrowed" teacher's scissors and accidentally cut off the tip of his finger, a decision was made to keep teachers' scissors under lock and key instead of in a cup on her desk. When those in charge read the accident report of how a removable metal center door frame insecurely fastened fell on the head of a first grade student causing the need for twenty stitches, the daily inspection of these frames was added to the maintenance check list. Are we getting the picture? Accident reports that are reviewed by appropriate personnel will insure that a onetime unavoidable accident does not repeat itself.

Much of what we are discussing is mere common sense, but it is surprising how we sometimes fail to think when in a new or emergency situation. Maybe another subtopic to this section should be "stop and think for five seconds before acting." When we do stop and think our decisions will usually be sound ones; decisions that first consider securing the safety of all of the students we are charged with before we consider that one student who may be in a life threatening situation. I am not making light of the life threatening situation, but it is important to make sure that we do not have two more situations before we take care of the one. In summary, in order to guard the physical well-being of our students, we must first be mentally and physically present when we are supervising; keeping our eyes on our charges at all time. Secondly, we must have an audible way of getting their attention, and finally, we must have a practiced plan of action in case of a serious emergency. As with most of the principles shared in this book, I have really told you nothing new. After having read this chapter, I know that there will be an awareness about guarding and protecting which in itself will help to insure the spiritual, soulish, and physical wellbeing of our students.

GUARDING AND PROTECTING OUR SCHOOLS

As we carefully and conscientiously guard and protect our students, we will of course be guarding and protecting our schools from legal liability. We live in a society that is frustrated and irritated with the loss of lives and well-being due to negligence and ignorance. The current legal system is quick to defend and to remunerate those who have been harmed. They are also quick to punish the offenders whether they acted with intent and malice or not. The court system will in 99 percent of the cases judge in favor of children over adults. These are the facts whether we like them or not. Therefore, we must do everything within our power to avoid these entanglements which easily put private schools out of business and, which without hesitation, land many well-intentioned teachers out of jobs and sometimes incarcerated. Let's discuss some simple and practical ways to help in this area. First, we must keep adequate records; second, we must have and follow rules; and lastly we must have proper screening of those who will be involved with children. As teachers, you may feel that these items are more the responsibility of the administration than yours, but again here I would like to emphasize that we teachers are in charge not of making policy, but of carrying it out. Therefore, let's discuss our role as we review these very simple principles which could lower our liability to almost zero percent.

RECORD KEEPING

It is important to keep accurate and sufficient records of things such as attendance, academics, discipline, communications, and any other major unusual situation which occurs with our students. Many teachers feel that keeping accurate attendance records is a waste of time. These accurate records could protect our school and ourselves against many un-founded cases of malpractice and other liabilities in which we are being sued because a student did not learn. Maybe this is because he never came to class, or because he was so tardy that he missed most of the instruction. Accurate attendance records can also protect us against allegations which supposedly occurred at a time or on a day when the student was not in class. Get my point?

We must also keep accurate and sufficient academic records. Some teachers grade very subjectively and sometimes grades do not accurately reflect the knowledge and understanding that a student has acquired, or there are simply so few grades that a student cannot succeed because they did poorly on the one test that was given in the entire quarter. Giving or not giving grades, and the effectiveness or need of using them has been an ongoing discussion in education since the beginning of formal schools. I strongly believe that though they do not reflect the wisdom (application of the knowledge acquired), they are necessary in determining whether or not our students really got the knowledge and understanding which we taught. I also strongly believe that a minimum of one grade per week determined without the use of notes, review sheets (test or quiz) is necessary. Though I feel that homework and other assignments which students do with the assistance of books, classmates, or even parents should be graded occasionally, since they are for practice, I do not feel that they should be a major part of the final grade a student receives unless they are allowed to correct these practice assignments for credit. I am very much opposed to grading on a curve, and also to giving bonus points so that students could have higher than a one-hundred on any assignment. This could be a chapter in itself, and here we are talking about legally protecting ourselves and our schools so I will get to the point. Honest, integrous, and sufficient evaluations and respective grades will protect us from allegations of malpractice because our students made excellent grades, but could not pass a simple math college course or write a college paper. Get my point?

It is crucial that we also keep good records regarding matters of discipline. Since we deal with so many issues, it is always difficult to remember exactly what did occur; therefore keep notes on serious matters of discipline requiring any action beyond a single verbal correction. Most schools have forms to complete when serious disciplinary action is taken such as detention, suspension, or expulsion. It is wise to keep a copy of these forms and other discipline notes in an informal file. Of course the school will keep major and official discipline forms in the student's permanent file. In addition, I recommend that a disciplinary communication sheet either in our computer or on a hard copy be posted each time we correct students beyond a mere verbal warning. We want to include the who – name all involved; the when – include the date, day, and time; the where – classroom, playground, or restroom; the what – a brief description of the event and the student's response to correction; and finally the action taken. These notations will take only a few minutes to complete, and are very helpful as we work with parents to train our students in behavior that respects the rights of others.

Our discussions with parents should also be documented on what I call a Parent Communications form (Sample #8 – Communications form). This form should include the student's name, date and type of communication (phone, email, meeting), persons involved or present, issues discussed, actions taken, and follow-up date if one is necessary. Again, due to the volume of students which we teach, it is easy to forget who we have talked to and what we have agreed on, or even the fact that we discussed a matter with a parent. I always like to give the parent a copy of the communication if we have agreed to take specific steps of action or if we will have a follow up conversation or meeting.

Finally, we want to document and keep records of any abnormal or out of the ordinary situation with any student. This note should also include the who, when, where, what, etc.... Some examples of this type of record would be behavior that was not common for a student on a particular day; unusual injuries (bruises) breaks in skin, lumps, bumps etc...which might indicate some sort of physical or mental abuse or neglect. I will take a side track here to mention what is normally made very clear regarding reporting to the appropriate authorities. We must personally and immediately document and report to the appropriate authorities any items in which we have concern that a child has been emotionally or physically abused or neglected. Though it is policy in most schools to report any abnormalities to the school principal, the individual who observed the situation must file the report with the state authorities. We should report unexplained injuries, unexplained changes in behavior or mood, concerning statements told to us in confidence, etc... If we fail to do so, then we are held responsible and even liable for what has happened to the child. I have found that the authorities do not act rashly or harshly when possible abuse is reported, and that records are kept to prevent abuse from continuing. Because we are concerned with guarding and protecting our students, we must consider their well-being above the reputation or inconvenience of the parent. We are not obligated to tell the parents that we have filed a report, and our reporting is always kept in strict confidence.

ESTABLISHING AND FOLLOWING RULES

In addition to keeping good records, establishing, implementing and following rules will help guard our schools from legal liabilities. Of course our main concern is not staying out of court; it is guarding and protecting our students. When we have established rules or policies and procedures, that are actually implemented and followed, we not only insure every student equal and just treatment, we have a common set of guidelines for dealing with every type of situation – academic, social, disciplinary, extracurricular etc... Therefore, every school should have a student and parent handbook which describes the rules or policy for dealing with admissions, attendance, grading, discipline, extracurricular activities, etc... These policies must be reviewed by the staff, parents, and students annually. Each staff member, parent, and student should sign a release stating that they have read and are in agreement with these policies or rules. Of course, it is of no value to have a beautiful handbook or policies and procedures manual if the rules are not implemented and followed. For this reason, each staff member must commit to following and enforcing the rules that have been agreed upon. When or if one or a few do not follow the policies, students can suffer injustices, and the school can become legally liable. Here is an example which we have all encountered. Maybe there is a rule that students will not be allowed to eat or drink in the classroom. One teacher decides that they will be the "nice guy" and allow it. The other teachers now become the "bad guys" who are trying to enforce the rule, and carry the extra burden of struggling with students who are allowed to do it in Mr. "Nice Guy's" classroom. Discrimination charges could arise because one student is allowed to break the rule while others are not, and so on. Therefore, it is the responsibility of each staff person to know the rules, enforce them, and to report those who are not following them. How about that teacher who insists on being the "buddy" of their high school students, who drives a group to lunch off campus without the permission of their parents. On the way an accident occurs, and not only is that one teacher liable, but the entire school is liable because other teachers knew of this mal-practice and did not report it. When we have set rules, which are communicated to those who must enforce them and to those who must follow them we are half way to guarding our schools from legal liability. As we are careful to implement and enforce those rules and even report those who do not follow them, we can help keep our schools' legal liability to a minimum.

PROPER SCREENING OF EVERYONE WORKING WITH STUDENTS

I will be brief regarding this final point of guarding and protecting our schools because it is mainly the responsibility of the administration to screen carefully all staff members and volunteers working in schools. I mention it here to enlist the help of teachers in this very important area of guarding and protecting our schools and students. Sometimes we find out things about the backgrounds and history of our co-workers that the criminal backgrounds and reference checks did not catch. If we become privy to important background information, we should very discreetly and confidentially mention our knowledge (not hearsay) to our administrator. In addition, we must properly screen all and every person who we allow to be with our students; all volunteers, parent drivers, field trip assistants, and even classroom volunteers.

THREE CRUCIAL RULES FOR STAFF MEMBERS

I would like to include at this point some rules that every teacher should follow whether they are written in a handbook or policy manual or not. The first is to always keep proper respect and position. The teacher-student relationship must be guarded. We are not our students' friends or parents. We are their teachers. Not allowing our students to become our friends or pals or "buddies", not allowing our students to call us by our first names, not allowing them to hang out with us outside of school, etc... will preserve that healthy and safe teacher-student relationship and will guard both ourselves and our schools from legal liability. The second very important rule regards appropriate touching of our students. Though students need "meaningful touches" as mentioned in a previous chapter, we will always touch from the shoulder up. It is inappropriate and dangerous even for coaches to slap their players on the bottom as a means of encouragement. Let's give them "high and low fives" or give them a "side, from the shoulders up hug" instead. Finally, we should never be alone with a student. If for some reason the situation presents itself, move with that student to the doorway so that there is never any question about what is happening.

GUARDING AND PROTECTING "NEVERS"

→ Never leave students alone

→ Never handle students physically when disciplining them or touch a student in anger

→ Never, touch a student below the shoulder or hug a student front to front (use the side to side hug instead).

→ Never be alone with a student (no matter what age they are) in a room with a closed door, in a car, or any other place; a witness will always help to keep our actions and words correct, and save us in case of false accusations.

→ Never allow students to operate dangerous equipment or do dangerous things

→ Never take students to your home (not even groups of students)

→ Never threaten a student verbally or physically

→ Never tease or use sarcasm with students; they are literal and though you were "only kidding" your words can be used against you.

→ Never cross the line of student-teacher relationship; we are not their friends, peers or equals; we are their teachers.

In summary of this very important chapter, we must remind ourselves of the amazing responsibility to guard and protect our students – spiritually, soulishly, and physically. Though we are not omniscient, omnipotent, or omnipresent, we have the ability to guard and protect our students by first being aware of our awesome and sometimes difficult responsibility in these areas, and then by following the few, but vital principles which we discussed in this chapter. As we follow these guidelines, we will also help to guard and protect our schools from legal liability due to negligence or malpractice. We do all of this because we love our students and desire to see them fulfill their individual destinies and make a difference in their worlds.

APPLICATION (WISDOM)

1. *Write your own plan for guarding your students spiritually and soulishly which includes a statement of your goal and a plan of action for reaching this goal. Put it into action this week and note the changes in your students.*

2. *Assess your classroom and other areas of supervision for breaches in the in sight at all times principle. Make the necessary adjustments.*

3. *Assess your supervisory duty effectiveness. Do you take work out with you, hold parent conferences, tutor students etc... while on duty? Commit to giving your duty your undivided attention.*

4. *Review your school or personal means of getting the attention of your students; make sure that it is adequate; then elaborate one step further with it. For example, if you use a whistle to get their attention, add two blows meaning stop and look for teacher; three for run to the nearest open door.*

5. Write, teach your students, and practice an emergency plan for the classroom and playground in a scenario where one student has a life threatening emergency and you are the only person supervising students.

6. Develop or copy the forms for recording disciplinary and parental communications.

7. Evaluate the legal liability of your school and put together a plan which will lower the liability to 0%.

Chapter Ten

PARENTS, A THREEFOLD CORD CANNOT BE BROKEN

Key Points

1. *A Threefold Cord Cannot Be Broken.*
2. *Parents, Our greatest blessing or worst nightmare.*
3. *T.E.A.M. Together Everyone Achieves Miracles.*
4. *Communication: The Key to Great Parent Relations*
5. *Customer Service to our students and their parents.*

We have learned (knowledge) and understood (insight), and hopefully already begun to practice the first nine keys to successful teaching: the purpose – teach to impact the world one student at a time; the how – touching hearts to touch minds, preparing to teach, disciplining to teach, six steps to really teaching, and teaching with "pizzazz". We have also addressed the benefits of brain research to assist us as we teach, and learned some keys to reaching those exceptional students. We also learned how to guard our students and our schools through supervision. I could not end this book, though I tried, without adding this last practical and essential chapter on those wonderful parents of our students and how to make them our allies and not our enemies. For those of us who teach at the post-secondary level and have virtually no parental contact just put the word student in where you see the word parent in this chapter. Have you ever noticed what seems to be the constant negative relationship between many parents and their children's teachers and sometimes between teachers and students? Why is it that when we get a note, email, text, or phone call from a parent, we dread the communication or meeting instead of looking forward to it? Why is it that the parent also dreads responding to our requests for meetings or our phone calls and other communications? I believe that it is because we generally only find time to meet or talk when there is a problem. We rarely meet or communicate for positive reasons like giving our parents a good report, or just touching base with them regarding our effectiveness with their children. We rarely, if ever, work side by side with our parents as a team, or find the time to form a working relationship with them.

A THREEFOLD CORD CANNOT BE BROKEN

This issue of parents and teachers working together could truly be at least 50% of the solution to the problems in education today. Throughout the history of education provided outside of the home, and in many cultures, an enmity seems to have been created between teachers and parents and even teachers and students. I believe that we must address this issue by looking at the biblical responsibilities of both parties. From the beginnings of civilization, parents were responsible for teaching and training their children both in spiritual matters (Deut. 6:7-8) and in vocational matters. In general, children followed the same vocation as their parents. In our current societies and civilizations, this is not always the case, sometimes to the chagrin of a mother or father who would love for the children to take over the family business or practice. In addition, most parents do not feel qualified or do not desire to be their children's teachers. Therefore, they have been faced with the need to delegate some of the teaching and training responsibility to others – teachers, coaches, instructors, schools, etc... Those of us who teach must understand this delegation of partial authority to us by the parents. We are not the ultimate authority or responsible party in regards to education; we are surrogate and act in "locus parentus" or in place of the parents. As we understand this principle, we can act accordingly, and much more efficiently.

Since we as teachers act in "locus parentus", we should know what it is that the parent desires for his/her student. There are many general things that we can assume that they want; reading, writing, performing math calculations, etc.., and we cannot provide a private or individualized instruction program for each student, but there is much power in agreeing with and walking together in one accord with the parents of our students. Most of our students come with a parent; wisdom would be to meet them and find out what they know about their children and where they see their children going, and even committing to working with those parents to help their students get to that destination. Time spent at the beginning of the year finding out from our students' parents or students in the case of those who teach at the post-secondary levels; how we can best serve our students would be great preventative maintenance and save us much time later. Have you noticed that most ropes are made of the same materials, but that those which must do the greatest work are made with more than one cord? The bible states that a cord of three cannot be broken easily (Eccles. 4:12). This threefold cord is made up of our students, their parents, and their teachers. If we all work together, we will have success; and if we lack one of the three, still a two-fold cord is better than a one-fold cord; and if it is just us working, one cord is better than none!

To achieve this threefold cord, let the parents and students know that you care and are at their service to achieve their goals. Find out what they want, and work with them and not against them. If we know where they need to be in certain areas, convince them of the relevance of what we will be teaching in regards to their ultimate goals for this year or course. When they know that we want to form a team with them, we will begin to walk together and in the same direction. Imagine a three legged race in which one of the persons is going one way and the other another. This just will not work, but when the two or three in this case are united and stepping with their tied legs at the same time and in the same direction, they are bound to win!

PARENTS, OUR GREATEST BLESSING OR WORST NIGHTMARE

Imagine teaching a group of twenty-five to thirty students with the help of five to ten to even fifteen aides! This is the potential that we have if we learn to utilize those wonderful parents. They can be our greatest blessing and asset, or they can be our worst nightmare. Those parents who can see and point out what needs to be done in our classrooms and in our schools just need to be channeled to be part of the solution and not a part of the problem. Let's ask them how they feel we could solve a particular problem that they see, and let them lead in implementing that solution! Imagine again the varieties of backgrounds, expertise, assets, connections, etc... that are represented by this group of twenty-five to thirty parents! Find out what the assets are and capitalize on them. Some parents have the asset of time on their hands, others have financial assets, others have networks and connections with powerful people, others have expertise which your students could benefit by, and others have certain technological abilities which you could use! The keys are to know who they are, understand their desire to share this with your class, and finally to utilize their assets to benefit your class (knowledge, understanding, and wisdom). (Sample #6 – Parent Survey Form)

T.E.A.M. TOGETHER EVERYONE ACHIEVES MIRACLES

We have all heard of the Parent Teacher Association (PTA), and I do believe that many associations have a high degree of success connecting parents with their children's schools and offering schools some very much needed assistance with volunteers and fundraising efforts for projects that tax dollars do not cover. I would like to share with you the vision of an outstanding parent who decided to be a part of the solution by channeling parent criticism and dissatisfaction into actions that solved problems and converted those "problem parents" into great assets. Her name is Rose Ayoub. At the time, she had two students in high school, one in elementary, and one in pre-school in our small school district. Rose and her husband Amen would definitely qualify for induction into the "Greatest Blessings School Hall of Fame"! It all began when Mrs. Ayoub drove her children to school each morning and noticed that many parents stayed in the parking lot chatting after their children had begun their classes. She noticed that much of the "parking lot talk" was negative and critical of what was happening in the school. She decided to help those very caring parents put their energies into solving the problems that they saw by forming a parent organization called "T.E.A.M.", which stood for "Together Everyone Achieves Miracles". The purpose of TEAM was to provide an avenue of positive action for parents with certain concerns by putting their talents to work in a positive way. Basically, if a parent felt strongly about a deficiency in the school, they were given the opportunity to be a part of solving that deficiency. Their time was channeled into working on solutions instead of talking about problems.

I have had the pleasure of seeing this organization succeed in each of the school districts that I have been responsible for, and have also seen this organization thrive in schools in Latin America. The beauty of TEAM is that it can have as many arms as there are needs in a school. There can be an arm for fundraising, another for social events for the students, another for technology, another for student appreciation, one for teacher appreciation, one for science, another for athletics; the needs are the only limit to the arms of TEAM. Each arm has a chairman (usually the person who saw the need); each arm meets monthly, organizes a volunteer group, and presents their projects to the administration; each arm achieves miracles. One unique TEAM arm was the Parent Advisory Group (PAG). A parent felt the need to communicate with the administration more frequently and efficiently so that the voice of the parents could be heard and responded to. Each class had a PAG representative who brought input and concerns from the parents in their class to the PAG arm of TEAM. The PAG representatives met with the principal monthly and then communicated with the parents in their class. As a principal, I appreciated the input

and the help of the representatives who in turn communicated with the parent groups from each class. In another school, the Athletic arm of TEAM provided all of the athletic needs of the school except coaching salaries; this included parents who collected entry fees at games, parents who worked the concessions, parents who raised funds to purchase uniforms, equipment, and even a new gymnasium.... What a great blessing!

Now you may be thinking that you are just the classroom teacher and not interested in what is happening in the entire school, but this concept begins in one classroom and then spreads to the rest of the school. Let's say that we really would like to make our classroom instruction more relevant by taking it out into the community we live in, but bussing is expensive and driver's hard to get. How about an arm of TEAM called transportation, manned by professional, licensed, and trained drivers from our parent group who give of their time to take our students to a laboratory, an airplane manufacturing plant, state historical sites, etc...? Maybe we need hands to help us change bulletin boards or to organize student folders or file test papers. How about an arm of TEAM filled with parents who have time to give? I am hoping that you are beginning to see the great value of our parents! Let's make them our greatest asset! (See Sample # 7 – TEAM Arms and Responsibilities). And now, on to some practical "how to's" regarding truly communicating with our parents or students.

COMMUNICATION – THE KEY TO SUCCESS WITH PARENTS

Communication with our students' parents (or with our students at the university level) keeps us connected and thus insures that we are walking together of one mind and one accord with one another. This agreement is essential if we are to achieve those agreed upon goals for this year, quarter or semester. The threefold cord is strengthened and maintained as we communicate with our students and their parents. Someone once said, information is power, and I believe that power is multiplied exponentially when we share information with others. Though it is sometimes difficult to speak to each parent in person, I highly recommend that we communicate no less than weekly with each parent. This weekly communication will help us to avoid playing phone tag with our parents, or sitting in hour long meetings which are so difficult to set up due to both our and their busy schedules. We might be thinking, "Great, that is all I need, one more thing to do on a weekly basis!" I hope I can convince you that consistent communication with parents will save us hours and hours of time and headaches in the future.

THE SANDWICH EFFECT

Before getting in to the specific types of communication, let's discuss some keys to communicating effectively. Have you heard of the "sandwich" effect? We always want to sandwich some less pleasant news with some very positive news. In addition, we always want to end our communications on a positive note. For example, we would like to advise a parent that their student is not completing homework assignments. We begin the communication with some positive statements about the student, such as his or her great work in the classroom and attention to us during instruction, and even how interested he or she is in the current topic. Then we move to our concern. It is good to express the concern in terms of what we see or hear or feel or think. Then, we always want to move to what we want for the student, for the class, and for ourselves. Finally, we want to discuss and agree upon a plan of action which will help us to achieve those agreed upon goals. We always want to end communications on a very positive note, expressing our belief that we know the situation will improve due to our close working relationship with each other and with their son or daughter. Remember, bread, dressing, meat, lettuce, tomatoes, cheese, bread make a great healthy and nutritional sandwich. Most of us enjoy our sandwich with that delicious bread of our choice followed by some sort of dressing and vegetables, and don't forget the cheese! When we communicate, let's think of our sandwich, and use this effect on our audience (students, parents, administration, etc...).

COMMUNICATION REQUIRES SPEAKING, LISTENING AND UNDERSTANDING

We have all been asked the question regarding the tree falling in the forest and whether there is really sound if someone was not there to hear it fall. I do believe that if no one is listening (not just hearing), then no communication has occurred; similar to my philosophy of teaching – if no one is learning we did not teach. True communication requires speaking, listening, and a mutual understanding of what is being communicated. So, how do we insure that someone is listening, and that they are actually hearing what we are saying? I would also ask the converse to that question, how do we know that we are actually listening to and understanding (not just hearing) what a parent or student is saying to us? Communication is the process of one person sharing something with another in such a way that the other person understands correctly and accurately what the communicator is saying. In many of our communications with others, many things get in the way of this process – pre-conceived beliefs, negative attitudes, lack of focus, defensive-ness, etc... We can alleviate this common communication problem by literally placing ourselves in the "listening" or on the "speaking" side of the communication process.

Listening requires attending such that I can even repeat what the communicator is saying. This means that as a listener, I must be active and not passive. I can ask the communicator to pause while I summarize what I have understood. Once they have acknowledged that I have, and even adjusted my under-standing or perception of what was said, then as a listener, I may ask for further information. As we go back and forth; communicating, then confirming that the listener has truly understood our communication, then giving more information, we will actually accomplish our goal of truly communicating. Sometimes as the speaker, we do not want to be interrupted, we want to "let it all out" and then hear what the other person has to say. Sometimes "all" is too much, and because of this, the person we are speaking to misses the true meaning of our communication. It is so much more effective to allow our listener to be active and to insure that they are actually getting what we are saying. We might ask ourselves how we get others on this communication process with us. Since we know the process of a speaker and active listener and their roles of sharing, listening actively enough to summarize accurately what was said, confirming that what was said was understood, and sharing more; we can direct the process either with a parent, student, co-worker, or even family member.

To review the communication process, we use the sandwich effect starting with the positive observations, then sharing our issue very objectively by stating what we have observed, heard, or even felt. Next we stop to allow the listener to summarize or re-state what we have shared. When their summation is accurate, we proceed to express what we want for our student, our class and even ourselves. Finally, we can move to a plan of action for us, our student, and our parent. This will greatly assist as we endeavor to walk together with our students and parents towards reaching the goals which we have agreed on for this particular quarter, semester, or year.

At this point, we might be thinking that this process will be effective for face to face or voice to voice communications, but what about those written communications. It seems that we currently depend more and more on written and electronic communications, and rarely have opportunity to meet face to face. Because of this, we must insure that what we intended when we sent that text or wrote that email is understood. We all know that without the face to face or voice to voice communication, much can go wrong as the reader can add many twists to what we are actually communicating. Therefore, it is imperative that our electronic communications request a response. This response is the same as the verbal response would be of the listener when we are involved in face to face communication. We must request this response or the communication will be a one way street from us to our parents, and we will not know whether they got the message or not. At the end of each electronic communication, ask the reader to respond letting you know that they actually received the communication, and how they feel about it, and whether they can agree on the plan of action. Simply put, it could read as follows: Please acknowledge receipt and understanding of this communication adding additional comments by return text or email. This same format should be used for written (paper) communications with our parents to insure that our communication is not a one way street, but a two-way highway.

TYPES OF COMMUNICATION

As we mentioned before, it is better to plan weekly communications than to spend hours and hours correcting miscommunications, or simply communicating. I suggest a weekly written (electronic or paper) communication with students at the high school and university level or with parents of Pk through high school. It is always more effective and time efficient to address the entire group than to have to communicate with each parent or student individually. There is only one of us, but twenty to fifty of them. We might question whether our constituency is even reading or hearing our communications, and this is why we always request a response; an email or text acknowledging receipt and understanding, or their initials on a "sign and return" slip or on their students agenda or planner. This weekly "newsletter" should be very brief and to the point starting with the positives, giving information, ending with words of encouragement, and requesting some form of acknowledgement of receipt.

In addition, I highly recommend a phone call, text, or email a day to one parent so that each parent is reached personally at least once a month. This is demonstrates concern for customer relations (our students and their parents are our customers!) and effective preventative communication; it demonstrates in action our true concern and commitment to our partnership with the students and parents. Use the sandwich effect, be brief, and if you have nothing to say, just give a positive report. These communications help our parents look forward to our calls instead of dreading them and wondering what their blessing has done wrong.

As a form of daily communication, no matter what the age of our students, require a planner or agenda on which assignments and other comments are written. These can be electronic or can be a paper version. When in doubt of what the assignments are, or whether there is a communication from the teacher, parents can be encouraged to check this daily. With younger children, initials on the planner tell us that the parents are informed. With university students, there is a place to find all of our "beyond the syllabus" assignments and communications. Parents or college students can also communicate with us through this planner or agenda (electronic or paper type), as long as we commit to check it daily also. You might object to the time that it will require of both parents and teachers to check this daily, but again the five minutes we spend walking around the room or just checking our emails for parental or student replies or acknowledgements, will save us so much time in the long run.

Finally, I highly recommend quarterly face to face meetings with the parents as a group. These meetings would obviously have to be in the evening when parents are not at work, and they should be planned, brief, encouraging, informative, and should allow for parents to communicate with us in addition to us communicating with them. This monthly meeting should be relevant and even fun as we build relationships with our parents. A monthly door prize could be donated by one parent and won by the parent holding the winning ticket. A parent could provide refreshments each month. These monthly meetings should be organized for parents of students from pre-school to high school and with our university students too. Attendance should be voluntary, but rewarded (how about adding two points to the lowest exam score for attendance?). This group meeting saves us time trying to meet with each parent individually, and after the group session, we could schedule some individual sessions as needed.

With this suggestion, I may have stretched you beyond your limit. You might be saying, "Wait a minute, this is my family or personal time you are infringing upon!" To that I would respond that one problem or negative situation with one student will take not one hour but many hours to solve. The one hour per month I spend communicating with my parent group will save me many hours of meetings with them and me and my supervisor. You might also be thinking that the only parents or students who will actually come will be those whose students are not having any problems. This is usually the case, but we want to put ourselves out there for any parent or student who will avail themselves to this opportunity to communicate with us. And what of those parents who will try to seize the opportunity to attack or gain support against us or our methods or procedures? The fact that we are open and receptive and transparent will protect us from most "ambushes", and we will have other parents there who will help us to communicate with those who do not understand.

COMMUNICATION PLANNERS: A MUST

To end our conversation regarding communications, I highly recommend what I will term "Communication Planners". All communications outside of the ordinary with parents and students should be posted to a "Communication Planner". This is a simple electronic or paper version on which we can track and plan our communications with our students and parents. Because there are double of them to one of us which puts us at a ratio of teacher to parent and students of sometimes 1:60, it is important for us to document our out of the routine communications with them. Though we are brilliant and have great memory, we can sometimes confuse or forget what we said to whom and when. All the communications should be kept in one file and in alphabetical order for quick access. After an out of the routine communication, we should pull the file and document the communication. When we set a meeting, we should plan the agenda (sandwich menu). During the meeting, we can document the parent or student response and our (parent, teacher, and student) action items and follow-up date. We can also use these communication planners to note incidences of out of the ordinary behaviors of our students. They will make us efficient as we manage the students and parents who depend on us. (Sample #8 – Communication Planner).

I would like to end this brief discussion on communication with a few words regarding customer service. First, we must understand that the teaching vocation is one of service. Our first line of service is to our students; the second line is to their parents, and the third to our co-workers and administration. Sometimes we get the service lines reversed. When prioritizing our time, we must give the most time to our first line customers – our students, then to the parents, and lastly to our co-workers and administrators. Students must be first, parents second, and the demands of our school systems last. Many teachers complain about paperwork from the system that takes time from our students. When this happens, I suggest that we voice this as a concern, and strive to spend the majority of our time and efforts on our students and their parents. Let's remember that our students and subsequently their parents are our customers. Though education has not been established as a competitive free enterprise system like restaurants or other businesses, we should see our schools and classrooms as a business. Satisfied customers are key to the success of our "business", and a key to their satisfaction is frequent, clear, and effective communication.

Entire books could be and no doubt have been written on the topic of parents and teachers working together, but hopefully you have learned some very important keys to successful parent-teacher relations. First, we must form a threefold cord between us, our students and their parents so that we can walk together in agreement regarding the education of the students which have been assigned to us. We can get agreement by identifying the goals that each have for the season that we will work together. We must begin to see our students' parents as those ultimately responsible for the education of their students and then partnership with them to achieve their educational goals. Daily, weekly, and monthly communications will maintain our united partnership as information empowers. Parents should be our best asset and not our worst headache, and can be if we know what interests, assets, and experiences they have. As we help parents to convert their concerns into solutions, we will achieve miracles and especially the miracle of education.

APPLICATION (WISDOM)

1. *Have each parent complete a parent survey with the purpose of utilizing their expertise, resources, or time to enhance what you do in the classroom.*

2. *Meet with each parent to find out about their students and their desires for them, and to express your commitment to assisting them.*

3. *Discuss beginning a "TEAM" in your school with some faculty members and your school principal.*

4. *Begin a "Communication Planner" file to note all out of the ordinary communications with parents and students and to plan each meeting.*

5. *Personally call one parent a day until you have talked with every parent, then start all over again.*

6. *Publish a weekly newsletter.*

7. *Schedule monthly meetings with parents that are informative, fun, and that allow parents to speak too.*

CONCLUSION

In conclusion, I would like to encourage you as you teach to make a difference in the lives of your students. Called and chosen teachers may not do everything correctly; they may not know everything there is to know; they may not be perfect; but they do love their students and this love covers a multitude of errors and faults. Do your best as often as you can. Take your breaks and renew your strength and love for teaching. Continue to learn and endeavor to create new and interesting ways of presenting knowledge. Be a person who empowers others to do what they were created to do. And above all, enjoy the ride! You will be that person who transforms the world we live in by being a part of the transformation of your students. Congratulations!

CURRICULUM GUIDE/OVERVIEW TEMPLATE
GRADE SUBJECT
(Sample #1)

GRADE/SUBJECT:

TEXT BOOK(S):

GENERAL COURSE OUTCOMES:

GENERAL DESCRIPTION OF COURSE:

STATE ESSENTIAL ACADEMIC LEARNING REQUIRE-
MENTS (EALR's) AND GRADE LEVEL EXPECTATIONS
(GLE's) (State of Washington):

OBJECTIVES BY GRADE. TERM OR QUARTER. WEEK:

    Examples: 11.1.1: (Eleventh Grade. Quarter 1. Week 1 :)

                4.1.1: (Fourth Grade. Quarter 1. Week 1 :)
                     Students will identify nouns and verbs
                     in a sentence.

             PK.1.l: (Pre-school. Quarter 1. Week 1 :)
                     Students will write the letters "A" and
                     "m" and identify their sounds.

GENERAL DESCRIPTION OF METHODOLOGY/
CLASS PROCEDURES:

ASSESSMENT STRATEGIES AND GRADING:

COMMENTS: (Weekly posting regarding challenges, great
ideas, what worked and did not work field trip information,
guest speakers, etc...)

CURRICULUM GUIDE/OVERVIEW
(Sample #2)

GRADE/SUBJECT: 11th Grade Language Arts (American Literature, Composition, Grammar)

TEXT BOOK(S):
1. *American Literature* (3rd Ed.), Abeka Books
2. *Handbook of Grammar and Composition* (4th Ed.), Abeka Books
3. *Workbook for Grammar and Composition V*, Abeka Books
4. *Vocabulary and Spelling V*, Abeka Books

GENERAL COURSE OUTCOMES:
1. Communicate orally and in writing in a clear, correct, and organized manner.
2. Analyze American literature understanding historical, geographical, and author's influence on literature; communicate analysis in written format.
3. Increase vocabulary for usage in oral and written communications

GENERAL DESCRIPTION OF COURSE:
Literature: American Literature presents the great works of American poets, short story authors, essayists, and novelists through the 19th and 20th centuries. Students will read, analyze, discuss, and write about the works they encounter.

Composition/Grammar: The writing process—plan, write, rewrite, and edit will be used in the following types of writing: paragraph, paraphrase, précis, character sketch, type sketch, character analysis, classification, critical book review, exposition of a process, argumentative essay, essay answer, narrative essay, and research paper. Reinforcement of grammar principles will be Students will complete six book reviews and one research paper throughout the duration of the course. Students will learn how to apply grammar principles in composition. Approximately 8-15 minutes is spent on grammar daily.

Mastering **vocabulary and spelling** words will help the students in their expression and communication.

STATE ESSENTIAL ACADEMIC LEARNING REQUIREMENTS (EALR's) AND GRADE LEVEL EXPECTATIONS (GLE's) (State of Washington):

Reading: reading is purposeful and automatic. Readers are aware of comprehension and vocabulary strategies being employed especially when encountering difficult text and/or reading for a specific purpose. They continue to increase their content and academic vocabulary. Oral and written responses analyze and/or synthesize information from multiple sources to deepen understanding of the content. Readers have greater ability to make connections and adjust understandings as they gain knowledge. They challenge texts, drawing on evidence from their own experience and wide reading. Students continue to read for pleasure.

Writing: students write independently with confidence and proficiency. They explore, interpret, and reflect on a wide range of experiences, texts, ideas, and opinions. Students choose the most appropriate form of writing to achieve the desired result for the intended audience. As students persevere through complex writing projects, they write sophisticated, complex literary texts and/or organized, fluent, and well-supported nonfiction. Complex forms of punctuation are used accurately and grammar/language is manipulated to enhance writing. Vocabulary is carefully chosen to create vivid mental images or elaborate on ideas. Students maintain a portfolio or collection of their own writing and continue to regard writing as an essential tool to further their own learning in and beyond high school.

EALR 1: The student understands and uses a writing process.

EALR 2: The student writes in a variety of forms for different audiences and purposes.

EALR 3: The student writes clearly and effectively.

EALR 4: The student analyzes and evaluates the effectiveness of written work.

OBJECTIVES:

Example: 11.1.1: Junior Senior. Quarter 1. Week 1:
Students will review writing process.
Students will commence reading the Scarlet letter
Students will write journal entries for first three chapters
Quarter 1:

1. Grammar:
    11. l.1: Parts of a Sentence
    11. l.2: The Writing Process
    11. l.3: Essay Answers
    11.1.4: The Paragraph
    11. l.5: Sentence, Fragments, Run-on Sentences
    11. l.6: Parts of Speech
    11. l.7: Verbal's
    11. l.8: Sentence Construction
    11.1.9: Book Report
2. Composition:
    11. l.1-2: Paragraphs

11.1.3-4: Character Traits

11.1.5-6: Short Critical Book Review

11.1.7-8: Oral Book Review

3. Literature:

11.1.1-2: The American Spirit

11.1.3-4: The American Short Story

11.1.5-6: The American Drama

11.1.7-8: Early America

GENERAL DESCRIPTION OF METHODOLOGY/CLASS PROCEDURES:

Students will write in journals first five minutes of class; Fifteen to twenty minutes will be spent on discussion of literature;

Ten to fifteen minutes to review grammar; Five minutes to review spelling/vocabulary; Last 10 minutes dedicated to guided practice and writing; HW will consist of daily reading and weekly writing assignments

ASSESSMENT STRATEGIES AND GRADING:

HW/Quiz/ In Class Assignments 1/3; Formative Assessments 1/3; Final Exam 1/3

Minimum of one HW, Quiz, or In Class Assignment per week

Formative Assessment Weeks 3 and 6 and 9. (Major writing assignments & Tests)

One Final Exam per semester

Grading Scale:

A: 3.6 to 4.0

B: 3.0 to 3.5

C: 2.5 to 2.9

D: 2.0 to 2.4

COMMENTS: (Weekly posting regarding challenges, great ideas, what worked and did not work field trip information, guest speakers, etc...)

> 11. l.1: (11th grade. Quarter 1. Week 1 :)
>
> > 1. *Scarlet Letter* was discussed and presented by groups to enhance interest & insure reading.
> > 2. Students rusty on writing process.
> > 3. Guest Speaker "Nathaniel Hawthorne"

OVERVIEW/CURRICULUM GUIDE
(Sample #3)

GRADE/SUBJECT:

First Grade Reading/Phonics/Language/Spelling

TEXT BOOKS: <u>A Handbook for Reading; Letters and Sounds 1; Language 1; Spelling and Poetry 1</u>. A BEKA BOOK, Pensacola Christian College, Pensacola, Florida, 2000.

BIBLICAL BASIS: We must teach reading so that our students can fulfill Psalm 119:11: Thy Word will I hide in my heart that I might not sin against God. Phonics is the foundational stone to reading just as Jesus is the chief cornerstone in Christianity. God made sure that His message was written so that people could know what he said; therefore it is crucial that every believer be able to read. Phonics is a line upon line, precept upon precept approach to the decoding process.

God commanded Moses to write a copy of the Law (Deut. 17:18-20). Unless we know how to read, all of God's writings would be in vain.

OVERALL INSTRUCTIONAL GOALS:

Phonics: Students will learn phonics in six easy steps:
1. Recognize the short vowels and their sounds
2. Recognize the consonants and their sounds
3. Blend consonants with vowels
4. Sound one vowel words
5. Learn the sounds of long vowels
6. Learn the special phonics sounds.

Language: Beginning concepts are introduced

Spelling: Students learn one spelling lesson per week; lists coordinate with phonics lessons.

Poetry: Familiarizes students with good poetry through recitation and memorization

SCOPE & SEQUENCE/OBJECTIVES BY QUARTER:

QUARTER 1: Charts 1-9

QUARTER 2: Charts10-12; learn alphabetical order

QUARTER 3: Chart 13; homonyms; alphabetical order; prefixes

QUARTER 4: Adding suffixes, contractions; review of all topics

Students will:

Q1   Charts 1-9

1. Master short and long vowel and consonant sounds.
2. Learn and apply through decoding the one and two vowel rules
3. Find rhyming words
4. Learn and use the "-s" suffix
5. Learn to begin sentences with a capital letter and end them with a period
6. Learn to read and write compound words
7. Find opposites
8. Memorize one poem per month
9. Study and master vocabulary words and spelling words

Q2   Charts 10-12

1. Identify root words and syllabicate words
2. Double final consonants when adding a suffix

3. Drop silent "e" when adding a suffix
4. Learn alphabetical order
5. Memorize one poem per month
6. Study and master vocabulary words and spelling words

Q3   Chart 13
1. Learn prefixes and syllabication between prefixes and suffixes and roots
2. Practice alphabetical order
3. Learn prefixes
4. Learn syllabication between prefixes and suffixes and root words
5. Changing "y" to "i" before adding suffix
6. Memorize one poem per month
7. Study and master vocabulary words and spelling words

Q4   Review charts 1-13
1. Learn what contractions are and how to write them
2. Review all topics and charts presented this year.
3. Review all poems
4. Study and master vocabulary words and spelling words

INSTRUCTIONAL METHODS:

Schedule: 25 minutes is necessary for
               Phonics/Language/Spelling
               10 minutes is needed for Poetry and Story time.

Language: Concepts are introduced during phonics time, and practiced through a daily seatwork assignment. This assignment includes silent reading, creative writing and comprehension activities.

Spelling: Students learn one list per week; 5 minutes of phonics time is spent
Spelling these words.

Methodology: Phonics, Spelling and Poetry are presented in an oral drill and practice format. Drill must be fast, repetitive, varied, and exciting. Visual charts and cards are used extensively. Games are an important part of teaching phonics effectively (see teacher guide page 23 for some great ideas).

Homework: Spelling words are written once a week

EVALUATION/ASSESSMENT:

Grading: Phonics and Spelling Tests are given weekly; each test has equal weight.

Students are not graded on Language or Poetry in first grade

COMMENTS:

1. Animal Toss is a great game to use to practice spelling words; Call a word and toss the animal; student who catches the animal gets to spell the word and toss the animal to another student once the next word is given.
2. "When two vowels go walking the first was says his name and the other is 'sh-h-h-h-h' silent.
3. "A" says "a" as in apple, "A" says "a"-"a"-"a".
4. Each symbol and rule on phonics charts should be said twice. "sion in television, "s-i-o-n". then repeat again.

LESSON PLANS HS ENGLISH
(Sample #4)

	Supplies	Bible	World Lit. (10)	Themes In Lit. (9)	American Lit. (11/12)	Lang. Arts (6)
Monday		Discuss Ch. 3 "Honest Measures"— learning to allow God to be the only judge HW: complete in-class activity	GC: Continue learning rules of capitalization p. 7; introduce the writing process p. 230-231 VSP: review spelling words; teach vocab words 1-4 HW: Lit- read p. 9-13; question #2 p.10 and #1 p. 13 VSP-write spelling words 2x; vocab #1-6 1x	GC: Review manuscript form; teach rules of capitalization p.2 VSP: review spelling words; teach vocab words 8-10 HW: Lit- read p. 9-18 VSP-write spelling words 2x; vocab 8-10 1x	GC: Review the writing process; learn differences between phrases and clauses p. 4-5 Lit: discuss poem and essay p. 3-4 VSP: review list 1 for quiz next Friday HW: none	GC: Review subjects and predicates; learn how to diagram a simple sentence VSP: introduce list 1; teach vocab words 1-5 HW: GC: "Go Back" p. 10 VSP-write spelling words 2x; vocab words 1x and use in a sentence

	Bible	World Lit. (10)	Themes In Lit. (9)	American Lit. (11/12)	Lang. Arts (6)
Supplies					
Tuesday	Discuss Ch. 4 "Solomon's Search" – learning not to chase after material goods HW: complete in-class activity	Lit: *Reading Quiz; Discuss p. 3-8 &9-13 VSP: review spelling words; teach vocab words 5-8 HW: GC-complete composition from Mon. VSP-write spelling words 2x; vocab #7-12 1x	Lit: *Reading Quiz; Discuss p. 2-8 & 9-17 (Walt Whitman) VSP: review all spelling and vocab words HW: GC- p. 3 Ex A #6-10, Ex B #7-12; p. 6. Ex F VSP-write 1 original sentence for all vocab words	*Senior Mission Trip* Juniors- Joint Project with U.S. History: Research Paper	GC: Learn how to identify a compound sentence VSP: teach vocab words 6-9 HW: VSP-write spelling words 2x; vocab words 1x and use in a sentence

STUDENT AFFIRMATIONS
(Sample #5)

I can do all things through Christ who strengthens me
(Phil. 4:13)

I am willing and obedient therefore I eat the good of the land.
(Isaiah 1:19)

I am quick to listen and slow to speak, slow to take offense, and
slow to get angry. (James 1:19)

I am like a mighty man as I control my tongue and speak life
(Prov. 18:21, 10:20, 15:4; Psalm 39:1, 45:1)

The Holy Spirit reminds me of the things I have learned.
(John 14:26)

Everything that I set my hand to do prospers and comes to full
maturity (Deut. 30:9; Prov. 10:4)

I am a child without blemish, well favored, skillful in all
wisdom, cunning in knowledge, and understanding
science. (Daniel 1:4)

I obey quickly without questioning, doubting, faultfinding or
criticizing. (Phil. 4:14; Acts 10:20; James 1:22)

I am more than a conqueror and I have the victory through
Christ. (Rom. 8:37)

I have the mind of Christ (I Cor. 2:16)

I do not have a spirit of fear, but of love and power and of a
sound mind (II Tim. 1:7)

The Holy Spirit leads me into all truth (I Cor. 2:13)

I am diligent (Prov. 10:4)

I have the peace of God that passes all understanding
(II Cor. 13:11)

PARENT SURVEY

(Sample #6)

TEAM *(Together Everyone Achieves Miracles)*

Dear Parents,

TEAM is off to a rousing start as we come together to help support the administration, staff and students of _____, but <u>we need you</u>! To best use the gifts, talents and resources of you—our TEAM—we are asking you to provide us with your special skills, trade or occupation, and personal passions.

All information that you disclose is for use by the TEAM Executive Board only. A member may contact you to participate in various projects or programs depending upon your availability. The information will remain confidential and is for school related use only. We appreciate your cooperation and look forward to meeting and working with you throughout this school year!

Please complete the following form and turn it in to your child's teacher or to the school administration by **Wednesday, October 27, _____.**

Thank you!
TEAM Executive Board

NAME:	PHONE #1:
E-MAIL:	PHONE #2:

If you need more space to answer the following questions, please use the back page > > > > > >

1. Are you a business owner?	
2. What is the name of the business you own?	
3. What is the nature of the business you own?	
4. If you are not a business owner, what company do you work for?	
5. What is your occupation or job title?	
6. Please give a brief description of your current job position:	
7. Describe any special interests, skills or personal passions or hobbies you may have:	
8. Would you be willing to share your experience and expertise with our students?	
9. Do you have a relationship with any businesses that our school may contact for assistance or donations? Please describe:	

MEMBER ROLES AND RESPONSIBILITIES
(Sample #7)

TEAM (Together Everyone Achieves Miracles)

Role	Name and contact information	Responsibilities
President	Name and contact information	• Facilitate meetings and oversee organization and function of TEAM • Primary liaison between administration and parents
Vice President		• Facilitate meetings and oversee organization and function of TEAM in absence of president
Secretary		• Take notes and keep accurate TEAM records • Assist with TEAM communications
Treasurer		• Monitor and submit reports on funds received and spent by TEAM • Assist with secretarial tasks and duties in absence of the secretary
Athletic Boosters Chair		• Coordinate athletic fund raising efforts • Assist with obtaining donors and sponsors for athletics program
Blessed to be Blessings Chair		• Develop and coordinate school wide events intended to bless teachers and students
Faithful Servants Chair		• Recruit volunteers for various school activities and events • Work closely with class representatives and various TEAM arm chairpersons
Master Askers Chair		• Work with school fundraising coordinator to facilitate school wide fundraising events and development • Obtain gifts and funds from donors on behalf of the school
Media Marketing Chair		• Develop and coordinate school promotional activities and events

Role	Number	Responsibilities
Master Techs Chair		• Develop and coordinate events and activities that support and strengthen the use of technology in the school
Spiritual Warriors Chair		• Establish and coordinate prayer teams and special school related spiritual campaigns or functions • Ensure that school's prayer needs are covered in prayer
Wall Builders Chair		• Establish and coordinate work teams to assist the school to maintain and improve school facilities
Wisdom Builders Chair		• Develop and coordinate educational events or special speakers to enhance learning opportunities for students
Parent Advisory Group Elementary (K3-6) Chair		• Oversee and coordinate Grades K3-6 PAG class representatives • Share concerns with administration and follow-up with parents in event of PAG representative's inability to do so
Parent Advisory Group (PAG) Secondary (7-12) Chair		• Oversee and coordinate Grades 7-12 PAG class representatives • Share concerns with administration and follow-up with parents in event of PAG representative's inability to do so
Parent Advisory Group (PAG) Representatives	1 per class	• Meet regularly with school administration to share concerns and feedback from parents • Follow-up with parents to bring resolution to their concerns and feedback
Class Representatives	2 per class (more for larger classes)	• Serve as liaison between teacher and parents • Communicate information from TEAM to other class parents • Enlist help and involvement of other parents in the class

COMMUNICATIONS PLANNER
(Sample #8)

Student: _____

Attendees: _____

Date: _____

Communication type:_____

Agenda: (Bread, Meat, Bread) (Objectives)

_____

_____

_____

Communications:

_____

_____

_____

_____

_____

Action Items and Deadlines:

_____

_____

_____

_____

_____

Signatures:

_____

_____

KEY POINTS
(Sample #9)

Chapter One – Teach, Teach, Teach – What Is It and Why Do It?
Key Points
1. Teaching is not a profession or a job – it is a calling and a vocation!
2. Teaching requires learning – if my students do not learn, I have not taught!
3. Teaching has three aspects – knowledge, understanding, and the ultimate goal, wisdom: applying or doing what you learned.
4. Chosen teachers meet six requirements:
   a. They are willing (Here I am, use me.)
   b. They give their lives for their students.
   c. They are motivated by love and compassion for their students.
   d. They are taken captive by this vocation. (Teach or die!)
   e. They are prepared (Study to show themselves approved).
   f. They are anointed or are yielded to the "Master Teacher".

Chapter Two – Touching Hearts to Touch Minds
Key Points
1. Connecting and relating to our students by touching their hearts first, will then help our students to open their minds to what we teach.
2. External impressions of our internal qualities such as friendliness, professionalism, strength, courage, and wisdom will help our students want to learn from us.
3. We can establish a relationship of trust by seeing, speaking, and believing in what our students will be become.

4. Blessing our students with meaningful touches, spoken messages, expressions of high value and desire for a special future, and commitment will touch our students' hearts so that they will allow us to touch their minds.

Chapter Three – Prepare to Teach or Plan to Fail
Key Points

1. We either plan or prepare to teach, or we have planned to fail.
2. We must prepare annually ("Living Curriculum Guide"), weekly (Lesson Plan & Notes and Outlines), and daily (Meditation, Prayer and Positive Confession).
3. We are guides, facilitators, we show our students how.
4. We give our students knowledge and understanding with which they will be able to think and reason at the higher thinking levels.
5. We should always "MIS" and "KIS" (Make it simple and keep it simple)!

Chapter Four – Discipline, A Matter of Authority
Key Points

1. Good classroom management stems from an understanding of and an implementation of the principles of being in and under authority; we demonstrate our authority for others by submitting to them, we walk as people with the right and power to operate in authority, and in turn our students submit to our authority.
2. We should praise the students who do what is right and issue consequences to those who do wrong; thus those who do wrong should fear (healthily respect) us, and those who submit to our instruction are blessed by us..

3. We teach our students to do right, not just out of fear, but so that they can have the peace of a clear conscience.

4. Be ready to correct and reward when it is convenient and when it is not; when we feel like it, and when we do not; be consistent.

5. Excellent classroom management requires a balance of instruction, rewards and consequences.

6. Use love and logic when disciplining; discipline in love showing empathy for the student's situation, and encourage students to logically determine consequences of their choices and fulfill those consequences.

7. A prepared, interesting and dynamic teacher is a great deterrent of discipline problems.

8. We cannot teach our students if we cannot control them

Chapter Five – Six Steps to Success
Key Points

1. Inspire our students to get them ready to learn by praying for them, having them say positive things about themselves, sharing a wise saying, or giving them a brain teaser.

2. Review in a dynamic, fast paced and interesting way to re-establish what was taught yesterday and the day before and the day before and the day before.

3. Instruct by telling, showing and letting our students; keeping it simple; and guiding them in practicing what we have taught them.

4. Allow students to begin their independent practice in class and finish it at home to insure that they are applying what they have learned.

5. Review one more time at the end of class to make sure that those "bricks" are laid straight.

6. Bless the students and give them those "last words" that will stick with them until you see them again.

Chapter Six – Do It With Pizzazz!
Key Points
1. Teaching with "Pizzazz" means using everything we have to keep our students awake and engaged as we teach, because we cannot teach someone who is asleep.
2. We must use our personality (all we have, both internal and external) to gain and retain the attention of our students so that they can learn
3. Our method of delivering our subject matter must be memorable and unique, unexpected and captivating, visual and multi-sensory and practiced.
4. The curriculum we teach must be both challenging to our students, and proven to be relevant and useful in their current or future lives

Chapter Seven – Brain Research Made Practical
Key Points
1. Emotional security and well-being give our students optimal brain functioning.
2. Oxygen, proper nutrition and sufficient sleep produce strong brain activity.
3. The brain latches on to knowledge which is connected with previously learned concepts.
4. Music, rhythm and movement enhance our ability to learn.
5. There are at least seven learning modalities (multiple Intelligences), which can be utilized to help every student learn easier: verbal, logical, visual, musical, body, inter-personal, intrapersonal.

6. The "Primacy-Recency Effect" (PT1, DT, and PT2) helps us use optimal learning times within a class period to teach important concepts.

Chapter Eight – Everything You Need to Know About the Exceptional Learner
Key Points
1. "Exceptional" students are those students who are not like every other student, those that require a different type of attention and a different type of teaching, and those who have to overcome various barriers in order to learn.
2. Some of the most common barriers of learning are Attention Disorders in which students are challenged with focusing; Academic Skills Disorders where students are challenged in acquiring the three "R's" of reading, writing and arithmetic; and Developmental Language Disorders in which students are challenged with articulation, expression, and receiving language.
3. U.S. Law (Section 504 Rehabilitation Act of 1973) requires that students with diagnosed learning disabilities be provided equal access and opportunities to learn in public educational institutions.
4. Effective strategies for working with exceptional students will include the following: proper communication, social support, a routine environment, modified assignments and assessments, varied methods of material presentation.
5. There are specific strategies for students with attention deficits, for hyperactive students, and for students with other visual and motor processing delays.

Chapter Nine – Supervision – Guarding and Protecting Our Students and Our Schools

Key Points

1. We guard and protect our students spiritually by preserving their image of who they are.
2. We can protect the mind or the thinking of our students, the will or the desire to do of our students, and the emotions or feelings of our students.
3. We guard and protect the physical well-being of our students through supervision.
4. Effective supervision requires the presence and undivided attention of supervisors, an audible means of communicating or getting the attention of students, and a practiced plan of action in case of emergency.
5. As we carefully and conscientiously guard and protect our students, we will of course be guarding and protecting our schools from legal liability.

Chapter Ten – Parents – A Threefold Cord Cannot Be Broken

Key Points

1. A Threefold Cord Cannot Be Broken
2. Parents, Our greatest blessing or worst nightmare.
3. T.E.A.M. Together Everyone Achieves Miracles
4. Communication: The Key to Great Parent Relations
5. Customer Service to our students and their parents.

SUGGESTED READING
AND REFERENCES

Beals, Gerald. (1999). *Biography of Thomas Alva Edison.*

Caine, R.N., & Caine, G. (1990, October). Understanding a brain based approach to learning and teaching. *Educational Leadership,* 48(2), 66-70.

Ezzo, Anne Marie, & Ezzo, Gary. (2002). *Growing Kids God's Way.* Growing Families International.

Fay, Jim, & Funk, David. (1995). *Teaching with Love and Logic.* Love and Logic Press.

Glenn, Robert E. (2002, February). Brain research. *Teaching For Excellence,* 21.

Smalley, Gary, & Trent, John. (2011). *The Blessing.* Thomas Nelson.

Sousa, David A. (2000). *How the Brain Learns.* Corwin Press.

Tobias, Cynthia. (1999). *You Can't Make Me, But I Can Be Persuaded.* WaterBrook Press.

Vygotsky, L.S. (1978). *Mind in Society.* London and Massachusetts: Harvard University Press.

Wilkinson, Bruce H. (1994). *Teaching with Style: Applied Principles of Learning Series.* Walk Thru the Bible Ministries.

AUTHOR CONTACT INFORMATION

To purchase books, for more information, or to schedule
Sandra C. Carranza to speak, please contact:

Sandra C. Carranza

253-221-1598

info@keystoeducation.org

www.keystoeducation.org

NOTES

NOTES

NOTES

NOTES